INCIDENT 48

RAID ON A SOUTH COAST TOWN

1943

Angela Beleznay

This edition published in 2012 on behalf of Angela Beleznay
by Natula Publications, Christchurch, Dorset BH23 1JD
Reprinted 2012

© Angela Beleznay 2012

The right of Angela Beleznay to be identified as the author of this work has been asserted by her in accordance with the Copyright, Designs and Patent Act 1988.

ISBN 9781897887943

A CIP catalogue record of this book is available from the British Library.

All rights reserved. No part of this publication may be reproduced, stored in a retrieval system, or transmitted in any form or by any means (electronic, mechanical, photocopying, recording or otherwise) without the prior permission of the copyright holder.

This book has been written to preserve information for local history.

The main purpose is to establish the facts behind the raid on May 23rd 1943, to confirm the number of casualties, and trace the names of those killed that day.

Whilst every care has been taken to record available information, no liability can be accepted for any errors or omissions, nor should it be relied upon as a definitive listing of all those who died.

This book has been compiled from mainly primary source information, and the recollections of those present at the time. Where this information is in the public domain, the references can be found either in the text, or listed at the end.

CONTENTS

Page

Acknowledgments	5
Foreword by Maurice Shnider	7
Prologue	9
Images of pre-war Bournemouth	11-14
Introduction	15
The Raid	23
The Destruction Caused	29
The Conclusion	66
The Combatants and Aircraft	74
The German Strategy and Players	86
Reports and Reminiscences	
Metropole Hotel and Beales	99
4 Lansdowne Crescent	115
Madeira Court	119
Civilian and Civil Defence Dead	129
Military Dead	146
Images of post-war Bournemouth	164-166
Glossary	167
Bibliography and Acknowledgements	169
Photograph Accreditations	174

ACKNOWLEDGEMENTS

I wish to thank the Staff of the following for all their help: -

Bournemouth Central Library Heritage Section
Bournemouth Cemetery Office
The Bournemouth Register Office
Dorset County Records Office
Dorset Fire Service
The Commonwealth War Graves Commission
The American Embassy

My thanks also go to: -

Beales Publicity Department
George Scott and Sons Ltd (Funeral Directors)
Deric Scott (Funeral Directors)
Mr. J. Levesley of Friends of New Forest Airfields
The Aircrew Remembrance Society
Bournemouth Evening Echo
Mr. Chris Goss
Mr. G. Cockett
Mr. J. Wilson, Mrs R. Taylor
Mr. J. Gear, Mr T. Coleman
Members of the Hudd family
Mr. W. Wenger and Mrs Nippa

and all those who have contributed their help in the production of this book.

I gratefully acknowledge their permission to use the information they have provided.

Fl/Lt. Maurice Shnider DFC. R.C.A.F.

FOREWORD BY MAURICE SHNIDER

I have always regarded Bournemouth as one of my favourite cities. With its waterfront drives, lovely parks and a multitude of hotels it contrasted sharply to the small Canadian prairie town where I was raised. My marriage to a beautiful girl from the Bournemouth suburb of Winton gave us the opportunity to make a number of family visits after the war and on each occasion I couldn't help but reflect on a time when the R.C.A.F. represented a significant presence in this lovely city.

Virtually every Canadian airman who went overseas spent some time in Bournemouth which served as No. 3 Personnel Depot during World War II. A number of autobiographical books have been written by former military flight personnel and without exception there is always a paragraph or chapter on Bournemouth. There we awaited our posting to an Operational Training Unit or an active squadron, thus entering the most exciting phase of our young lives.

I am reminded that over 17,000 members of the R.C.A.F. were killed in the Second World War and I recall, with sadness, that it was in Bournemouth where I saw many of my friends for the last time.

I went on leave to Bournemouth shortly after the Luftwaffe attacked on May 23rd 1943 and the sight of the devastation affected me profoundly. Years later I read Joanna Codd's anniversary article in the Bournemouth Echo which inspired me to visit the military graves in the North Cemetery.

Over the years I have been favoured with correspondence from Ed Perkins, the Deputy Editor of *Bournemouth Echo*, Barry Needham, Spitfire pilot and Willy Wenger, whose late brother participated in the raid. I now have the opportunity to express my admiration for Angela Beleznay whose efforts as a historian have ensured that there will be an enduring tribute to the innocent victims of one of the tragic episodes of war.

Fl/Lt. Maurice Shnider DFC. R.C.A.F (Retd.)
28th April 2012

PROLOGUE

I have lived all my life in towns and villages on the Hampshire, Dorset border and grew up listening to the recollections of those who were here during the War. The description of thousands of troops lining the streets of Southampton waiting to embark on the D-Day landings and how the men were there one day and gone the next, leaving the streets empty, made a lasting impression on me.

When I was a child in the New Forest, the old wartime airfields were popular picnic places and, as we played, older friends and family members had engrossed us in stories of the activities that had taken place only a few years before. I found Bournemouth's "secret" wartime history and the enormous part it played in the war effort fascinating, so I started my research.

At the time of this raid, Britain was at war with Germany. The War was at its height, and there had been enormous losses on both sides. Young men and women from all over the world had either volunteered or were drafted in to fight.

In this book I have endeavoured to uncover a wide range of previously unpublished facts relating to the Air Raid of May 23rd 1943 and offer them in their own historical context without, as far as possible, a subjective commentary. The information contained in this book details events that caused loss of life, considerable damage and great distress. This is published to bring to the attention of a new generation the circumstances of a significant event which has not previously been explored in such depth and to honour those who died that day and remember all those who were affected.

Angela Beleznay
June 2012

Bournemouth Square 1935, showing Central Hotel

Bournemouth Square 1935, showing Bobbys

Shamrock & Rambler Garage, 1930s

The Metropole Hotel, Lansdowne 1900s

Bournemouth Square towards Old Christchurch Road, 1930s

Beales, 1931

INTRODUCTION

On May 23rd 1943 Bournemouth was the scene of a major Air Raid. Between the first Air Raid Warning Siren sounding at 12.54 p.m., the 848th in the town since the outbreak of the war, (there were to be two further warnings that day) and the all clear being given at 13.25 p.m., 22 buildings were totally destroyed 3,359 were damaged (37 of these later required demolition) and the streets of Bournemouth were strewn with the dead, dying and injured. When the siren sounded it gave only 5 minutes warning before the first bomb was dropped as the clocks prepared to strike 1.00 p.m. Within the space of a minute, the whole raid was over. This was the 48th incident to have affected Bournemouth, and its most devastating.

A letter from The Controller's Office to the Mayor, Aldermen and Councillors of Bournemouth, dated 18th November 1944 states the following:-

Casualties	Men	Women	Children	Total
Dead	29	42	6	77
Seriously injured	15	28	3	46
Slightly injured	76	63	11	150

One man was also killed when dealing with the demolition at Beales Department Store.

Property Damaged

Buildings totally destroyed	22
Buildings requiring demolition	37
Buildings seriously damaged but repairable	268
Buildings slightly damaged	2,640
Buildings glass only	514
Total	3,481

In total approximately 25 high explosive bombs were dropped, one aircraft was shot down and crashed with the bomb intact. One unexploded bomb is known to have been found in the grounds of St. Paul's School. 21 others detonated on impact. These fell in the following areas:-

Upper Terrace Road
Bobbys (The Square)
Beales
West's Cinema
The Metropole Hotel
The Central Hotel (Richmond Hill)
Keystone Garage Car Park (Exeter Road)
The Shamrock and Rambler Garage
Cotlands Road
248 Holdenhurst Road
Dean Park Road
Lansdowne Road
Queen's Park South Drive
Richmond Wood Road
Howard Road
Drummond Road

    Manor Road
    Vale Road
    Bethia Road
    Spring Road
    Cleveland Road
    A German plane with bomb intact crashed on
    The St. Ives Hotel, Grove Road.

It must be noted here that the figures given for the dead and injured only relate to civilian casualties, military casualties were kept secret due to reason of national security. The Bournemouth Register Office officially recorded 123 people as having died due to war operations that day.

The figures provided by the Register Office cover all those who fell within the jurisdiction of the Registrar. The count includes all Civilians and British and Commonwealth Military Personnel, but excludes the U.S. Military as they had their own procedures. The register shows 114 as having died in central Bournemouth, at The Metropole Hotel, The Central Hotel and The Central Gardens.

Several of those who died are recorded as being wives of service personnel. Further information from this source can only be obtained by purchasing the relevant Death Certificates.

However it has been possible to obtain most of the details of bodies recovered from other sources. These details can be seen in the chapters: -

Civilian Deaths
Military Deaths

On Tuesday April 15th 1986 Alderman Harry Mears wrote the following letter to The Echo (this is the full letter printed that day)

I have read with interest the various letters that have appeared in your paper in respect of the air raid on Bournemouth that took place at 13.00 hours on Sunday, May 23, 1943.

I was the controller of Civil Defence for Bournemouth on that tragic day and shall never forget it. We were only able to give a few minutes warning before the German 'planes swept in from seawards. Twenty-two bombs were dropped and exploded in ten different areas of the town. Some unexploded bombs were found later.

It being a Sunday, more people were in their homes than on a working day, and in the hotels packed with the members of the armed forces, dinner was being served.

Casualty reports came in so fast from the Warden Service that our fire, ambulance and heavy rescue teams were stretched to the limits. Help was willingly given by members of the armed forces and civilians. I can not praise the morale and courage of all too highly. Fifty-nine buildings were totally destroyed and a further 3,442 were damaged. The worst incident was at the Metropole Hotel at the Lansdowne where a direct hit resulted in many airmen being killed or injured.

Civilian casualties were as follows: - 77 killed, 46 seriously injured and 150 slightly injured. In addition, one of my men was killed during demolition work at Beales.

*The number of military casualties was kept secret at the time for reasons of national security and each unit reported its own casualties direct to the War Office. The final figure for that day of all nationalities including American came to **131**, so with the addition of the **77** civilian dead the total was **208**.*

I can not mention all those who worked through that day and the next as there were too many, but they all showed a complete disregard of their own safety and their team spirit was magnificent. It is a great pity that we cannot recreate today that feeling of comradeship and caring that existed when people were under pressure during the war.

This was Raid Number 48 on Bournemouth and the town was to have three more before the war ended. I sincerely hope that future generations will not have to endure such senseless destruction of human life. My book which will contain the history of Civil Defence in Bournemouth from 1935 to the end of war in 1945 will be published this year. Further details of this raid and many others will be included.

Ald. Harry Mears, 26 Ocean Heights, Boscombe Cliffe Road, Bournemouth.

If these figures are accurate, 89 service personnel are unaccounted for.

Note: Alderman Harry Mears's book was never published.

Extracts from his unpublished typescript covering the period of this raid can be found in the chapter "The Destruction Caused".

Over the years many different figures have been quoted. It has been documented that 31 trainee British and Commonwealth Airmen died and 3 were reported missing. On November 10th 2000, Dr. Maurice Shnider DFC, a R.C.A.F. veteran wrote an article in the Winnipeg Free Press, entitled "Recalling Fallen Comrades". In this article he stated that 51 servicemen were killed that day.

The R.A.F. Operations Book for No. 3 PRC entry for that day states that 33 Airmen were killed and 2 were reported missing believed dead. Many others were injured.

A Home Office document dated 25th May 1943 and originally classified as SECRET, provides the information that 123 were reported dead, 50 seriously injured and 150 slightly injured.

Photographs of the Cumberland Hotel
taken by Lt. L Wenger

Photographs taken during the raid on Bournemouth
by Lt. L Wenger

THE RAID

The raid on Bournemouth was one of the notorious "Tip and Run" raids carried out by the Germans in this period. These were audacious, quick, low level raids, using light, fast fighter-bombers crewed only by the pilot. In this case the aircraft came in at approximately 50 feet over the sea, to avoid the radar. This raid occurred almost simultaneously with one on Hastings. The raid on Hastings only being four minutes earlier. The aircraft involved in these raids were Focke-Wulf 190(A-5) from SKG 10. It should be noted this Gruppe had recently been re-designated, and this was its first action since their re-assignment.

26 aircraft from IV/SKG 10 carried out the raid on Bournemouth. The initial official report stated 22, however this figure was later amended. Collier's *Defence of the United Kingdom* states 26 aircraft, with 25 bombs being aimed, 22 hitting their targets, a success rate of 88%. This figure is confirmed from other sources.

These aircraft were based in Caen - Carpiquet in France, just a short flying distance away. The aircraft took off from France at 12.30 p.m., arriving at Hastings at 12.56 p.m., and in Bournemouth at about 1.00 p.m. By 1.35 p.m. they had returned to base.

The FW190 Orders of Battle for IV/SKG/10 show the Commanding Officer at that time to be a Major Schumann.

Mrs Drew (left) and Mrs Seaton
in the burnt out kitchen of the St. Ives Hotel

The remains of Uffz. Schmidt's FW190

On the 17th May, they had 30 aircraft, of which 23 were recorded as serviceable. If as most reports show, 26 aircraft took part in the raid, then either three aircraft were repaired or borrowed from another squadron to make up the numbers.

20 aircraft from II/SKG 10 attacked Hastings. Two of these aircraft were lost in the raid.

In Bournemouth it was originally reported that two aircraft had been shot down, one having been brought down by machine gunners on the roof of Beales and crashing into the sea. It was seen to be "disappearing towards the sea and losing height". A young German pilot, Uffz. Eugen Streich, was killed when he crash landed on his return to France. The German records show only one aircraft being recorded as missing, piloted by Uffz. Fredrich-Karl Schmidt, aged 21 years. This had been his first operational flight.

The newspapers first recorded him as having been shot down by a Spitfire, but it was later reported that his plane had been brought down by machine gun fire in the region of the Pier. In the official report he is recorded as having been shot down by the gunners manning a machine gun post on the roof top of the East Cliff Court Hotel.

Uffz. Schmidt's plane crashed into the St. Ives Hotel, 34 Grove Road, landing on the flat roof with its bomb still attached. The bomb separated from the plane, which caught fire, setting the hotel alight. A photograph shows Mrs Drew and Mrs Seaton standing in the hotel's burnt out kitchen, with the remains of the FW190 engine in the foreground. At the time the St. Ives Hotel was being used as a hostel for the A.T.S. girls, none of whom were injured. (see chapter Reports and Reminiscences)

Cpl. Bill Hurley and his team had been ordered to R.A.F. Hurn to transport a Mustang engine. They were diverted to remove the plane wreckage at the St. Ives Hotel and Hurley gave this eyewitness report: -

The plane appeared almost undamaged, and with the crash, had imbedded itself in the flat roof, at an angle of about 45 degrees. The bomb was some 15 to 20 feet away embedded in the one of the supporting posts of a double garage. The Bomb Disposal officer tried to make it safe, however 45 minutes later it exploded, destroying the remains of the plane, and nearby house.

No reference could be found in the Bournemouth Register of War Dead to anyone having died in the subsequent fire in the St. Ives Hotel, nor is anyone on the Civilian List of War Dead listed as having died in Grove Road. However the Home Office record two people as having died at the address. It can only be assumed therefore that one was Uffz. Schmidt and the other may have been a military death.

Uffz. Schmidt was originally buried in the North Cemetery, as an "Unknown German Airman". He was eventually identified in 1947, and in 1963 his body was exhumed and re-buried in Cannock Chase, in Staffordshire.

The radar station at St. Boniface Down on the Isle of Wight had picked up the approaching aircraft on the chain home low radar as they crossed the horizon, mid Channel about 40 miles away, and Fighter Command at Middle Wallop had been alerted. With the simultaneous raid on Hastings, the 46 aircraft attack on the south coast would have severely stretched the defences. The fighters were up. The Spitfires from R.A.F. Ibsley had been scrambled; however they were unable to intercept the raiders before they reached the town. It has been described how a flight from 616 squadron at Ibsley was scrambled in response to the raid, made distant visual contact, but did not engage.

The FW190s, at low level would be capable of cruising at 280mph, and would probably have been only 7 minutes away from the Isle of Wight when detected and only about 11 minutes flying distance from landfall at Southbourne, giving very little time for warning.

The bombers had headed in from an east- south-easterly direction, at approximately 50 feet, with the sun half behind them. It was a sunny day, with a little cloud. They flew in over Boscombe and Southbourne, fanning out to cover four areas of the town, before exiting over the sea in the Branksome/Sandbanks area. On their way they dropped approximately 11 tonnes of high explosive bombs on the town, rising to a height of approximately 150-200 feet to do so. According to the official report at that time, the raid was over in a minute.

It may be of interest to note here that it has been quoted in previous reports, that the raid consisted of both Focke Wulf 190 fighter/bombers, and Messerschmitt 109 fighters. It has been said these were identified by the Royal Observer Corps at the time of the raid. Fighters did occasionally accompany bombers on raids as escorts, and it may have happened in this case, although so far no evidence has been found to confirm this.

THE DESTRUCTION CAUSED

Bombs exploded over ten areas of the town, with the worst damage and highest death rate occurring within the centre of the town itself. The bombers approached the town along the railway line, dropping bombs on the way, before fanning out.

A bomb falling in Dean Park Road, caused damage to property in both Dean Park and Littledown Roads. Richmond Wood, Howard and Egerton Roads were also affected, as was Queen's Park South Drive, by three bombs dropped in this area, with civilians being killed in Richmond Wood and Howard Roads.

In Springbourne, bombs fell in Bethia, Spring, Holdenhurst and Cleveland Roads, causing damage to the surrounding areas including Methuen and Windham Roads as well as Garfield Avenue and again with some civilian loss of life.

In the Boscombe/Springbourne area, properties in Carlton, Vale, Spencer and St. Clement's Roads were damaged by a bomb exploding in Vale Road. Number 38 Carlton Road was a children's hostel for evacuees; here the matron Julia Hartin lost her life whilst trying to rescue the children. A little boy, Roger Woollard, aged 4 years also died.

Drummond, Hamilton and Carysfort Roads were damaged by a bomb exploding in Drummond Road. Here a mother,

Florence Hawke and her two children aged 8 and 10 years and a gentleman called Henry Eggett aged 73 years, all died at number 54 Drummond Road, others died next door at number 56.

Manor and Grove Roads were also hit by bombs, with one death being recorded in Manor Road.

Some of the injured were taken to the Royal Victoria Hospital in Boscombe where they later died of their injuries.

The Royal Victoria Hospital, Boscombe

As the bombers approached the town, they dropped a bomb in Cotlands Road. This damaged properties in both Cotlands and York Roads. They then bombed the Shamrock and Rambler Garage, The Metropole Hotel and Lansdowne Road, thus affecting Holdenhurst, Oxford, Lansdowne and St. Paul's Roads.

Bomb damage, 252a- 256a Holdenhurst Road

Shamrock and Rambler Bus Garage after the raid

Bomb Damage at Bobby's, The Square

Old Christchurch, Fir Vale and St. Peter's Roads were next, along with Gervis Place, with bombs falling on West's Cinema and Beales department store. Upper Terrace, Exeter Road, The Square and Richmond Hill all suffered damage with bombs falling on Upper Terrace Road, Bobby's (in the Square, now Debenhams), The Keystone Garage Car Park in Exeter Road, and The Central Hotel in Richmond Hill.

Damage to property was extensive, and many were in a dangerous state. Several of the roads were unapproachable, and it took weeks before some of the roads, including The Square would be open to proper traffic. In the town, blast damage was severe, with the streets deep in broken glass and debris. Fifteen buses were destroyed when The Shamrock and Rambler coach station was hit. Two of the employees, George Adlem and George Walton were killed, their bodies being found in the wrecked offices. Further down the town, the buses parked in the bus station in Exeter Road had their windows blown out. At Bobby's, the bomb entered the front of the building on the second floor, went straight through the shop and exploded in the basement that was being used as an air raid shelter. Luckily it was empty at the time. Michael Hodges was having lunch in the restaurant at the time, and his recollection of the events can be read in the chapter Reports and Reminiscences.

It was however higher in the town where the greatest loss of life and structural damage occurred. Harry Mears gave the following description in his memoirs of what greeted him when he left the control centre that day:

> *It was nearly an hour after the bombing before I was able to leave the control centre in the town hall and visit the areas most affected. The sight that met my eyes as I crossed the Square and went into Old Christchurch Road was like something out of Dante's Inferno. Beales departmental store was engulfed in flames rising to a great height above the building, fireman playing their hoses onto the front of the building ran a great risk from collapsing walls and from overhanging debris. More hoses were played into the centre of the fire from the roofs of nearby buildings and desperate attempts were being made to prevent the fire spreading to other buildings. I had to step over shattered glass that littered the area and spoke to the fire officers on the spot.*

Beales store received a direct hit. The bomb caused the gas main to rupture and the ensuing fire engulfed the whole building.

So fierce was the fire, that it crossed the road and spread to J.J. Allens' Department Store, other surrounding buildings were also damaged. Sparks from the fire set light to the louvres of the belfry in St. Peter's Church, and threatened the timbers. The fire in the church was extinguished by members of the congregation and service personnel using stirrup pumps and buckets. It took them two hours to make the building safe. Later when the fire at Beales had been brought under control, the Fire Service turned the hoses on the church to "dampen down" and prevent any further burning.

Bomb damage, Beales May 23rd 1943

Bomb Damage, Beales May 23rd 1943

Clearing debris from Beales

Fire Brigade hoses and pumps, Bourne Stream Bournemouth

Beales corner showing 6" steel pipe
providing water for the Fire Brigade

Fifteen pumps from a number of towns arrived just to fight the fire at Beales and it was not until 17.00 hours that the fire was brought under control. It was reported in the newspapers following the raid, that it was the first time the local National Fire Service had been brought into operation in blitz conditions.

Within 30 minutes of the fires starting, the Chief Regional Fire Officer, the Fire Force Commander, and the Assistant Fire Force Commander for the area were all on the scene. With five major fires in the town, it was an enormous undertaking to bring them all under control. In addition to the fire at Beales, the other four major fires each required four pumps and crews to fight them, and there were eight smaller fires each requiring the attendance of a pump and crew. The Fire Service was assisted by the many military personnel in the town, who were later formally thanked for their help.

Water to fight the fires in the area of Beales was brought up from Bourne Stream using fire hoses and pumps laid out through the Gardens. This was stored in canvas dams around the burning building. Each dam contained 500 gallons of water and these were kept full throughout the day. Ted Hughes, one of the men fighting the fire that day, reminisced in his book *Bournemouth Firemen at War*: -

It was said that we could have floated Beales out to sea. I could not get near to get effective jets near the building because of the heat, but as my orders were to try to hold it from the nearby Arcade, I took crews up on the roof of the shops at the rear of Beales in Gervis Place. There I was able to place branch-men with one inch jets directed across the road, straight into the upper floors. Another crew were playing jets into windows where Beales adjoins the Arcade, which proved successful. Once I had established this, I went into the street, which was running with water and filled with debris and tangled lines of hoses.

The building was in a very dangerous state, there was a crack running through the brick work on the front of the building and all the lower floors were on fire. By the time the fire had been extinguished, the whole building had collapsed.

Another one of those helping to fight the fire at Beales that day with the Bournemouth Auxiliary Fire Service was 17 year old schoolboy Geoffrey Cockett. Geoffrey was an evacuee from Southampton who had first joined the service at Poole District Fire Station in 1940 at the age of 14, where he was trained as a part-time messenger/fireman. He recalls the following: -

I was billeted at 15 Hillcrest Road in Upper Parkstone at the time, and on hearing of the bombing in Bournemouth, immediately cycled to the town. Here I went to the fire control vehicle near Beales store. The store was a mass of flames. I was ordered to take over the task of directing the water from a hose branch onto the fire, this I did for over an hour before another fireman replaced me. Thereafter I waited near a group of firemen alongside a battery of several rigidly fixed hose branches, seeing the fire gradually being brought under control. It was the early evening before I cycled back to Parkstone.

Geoffrey is thought to be the bare headed man in the centre of the group of firemen seen in the photograph fighting the fire at Beales. The other firemen had steel helmets and Geoffrey was hatless that day. The height and hair style of the man in the photograph also matches Geoffrey's description at the time.

There was one fatality at Beales, that of Home Guard Douglas Herridge, who was killed by falling masonry. A member of the A.R.P. Rescue Service was also killed outside the Metropole Hotel by falling masonry, and William Henry Brown, the Head Warden died at Howard Road. He was buried on the 27th with the Union Jack draped over his coffin, his white steel helmet placed on top.

A Royal Marine was also reported as having been killed in the town by falling masonry whilst carrying out demolition work with the Home Guard. This may have been 2nd Lieut Peter Guy Francis, aged 20 years and is recorded as having died the following day at Boscombe Hospital.

Gunners from the 87th Light A.A. Regiment Royal Artillery, based in Poole, were manning an anti-aircraft post on top of Beales flat roof when it was bombed. Two of the soldiers were injured when their gun received a direct hit with cannon fire, they were evacuated through the smoke and flames first. However Lance-Bombardier Norman Lawrence and Lance-Bombardier John Howard, continued to fire at the enemy with their guns after the building was damaged, hitting an exiting enemy aircraft that was seen departing from the town, flying low out over the bay. The NCO's then led their men to safety through the fire, carrying their guns with them. For this they were both awarded the British Empire Medal for bravery on November 1st from King George VI.

Further along from Beales, in St. Peter's Road, where The Burlington Arcade is now situated, stood West's Cinema and Cairns House. Cairns House was being used as the Bournemouth Chamber of Trade Offices at the time, with flats above. West's Cinema received a direct hit, and Cairns House was badly damaged and required demolition. Two deaths are recorded as having occurred at Cairns House. Hotel Assistant Dorothy Kent Candy, aged 47 years, the widow of Major R.G.L. Candy of the R.A.F. died together with Michael Geoffrey Wheeler, who was aged 21 months. He is recorded as being the son of Maurice Henry and Valerie Wheeler. Their bodies were recovered on the 29th May. They are buried together in the North Cemetery. Mrs Wheeler's maiden name was Candy, and it is possible Dorothy Candy was the child's grandmother.

The greatest loss of life occurred at the Central Hotel on Richmond Hill. The restaurant and bar had been packed with people at the time. The hotel received a direct hit and much of this popular lunch time meeting place was almost obliterated. The secret report sent to the Home Office states that 54 people died here.

Ruins of Punshon Memorial Church and Central Hotel, Richmond Hill

7 airmen, all listed as being in the Royal Australian Air Force, and 28 civilians are known to have died in the Central Hotel. Some of the bodies recovered appeared to be unmarked, they had died of shock. Others dug out alive, later succumbed to shock and injury, with some dying in the ambulances on their way to hospital.

The true loss of life here may never be known for it is thought some of the bodies were unrecoverable, the damage was so great. All that remained was a pile of rubble.

The servicemen and women in the town, along with the civil defence workers and civilians, started to clear the rubble with their bare hands in attempts to rescue those buried alive. Many were brought out, including the hotel proprietor, however his wife, Nellie was killed. One woman was brought out alive the following day.

Harry Mears described the situation as follows: -

I then proceeded to the Central Hotel on Richmond Hill and received reports from the rescue squads and police at the scene.

Servicemen and civilians were working side by side with the rescue squads and were pulling the rubble aside with their bare hands. Sometimes they would stop to listen for sounds from trapped people and then the work would start again. Human chains were formed passing the debris from hand to hand, parties of men clambered over the wreckage, by arduous and extremely dangerous work they managed to release trapped people who were lowered to the First Aid staff waiting below with ambulances.

Rescuers toiled all day and into the night to search the wreckage of the Central Hotel and the Metropole Hotel where many had been killed. At the Central Hotel they had just begun to serve lunch when the bomb struck and wrecked the buildings, there was no fire and rescuers were joined by passers-by all digging furiously in the rubble. The chef of the Hotel had a lucky escape as he found a gap in the wreckage above him and got out through a basement window, he was Mr. Herbert Nicholls. The porter George Cook and the kitchen maid Mrs. Norman got out the same way. Miss Elsie Barritt, waitress, who had just served a customer in the restaurant got out alive as did the lady she had been attending. Rescued and rescuers alike were covered in dust and grime that got into their throats and eyes.

There had been a meeting in the town of the Civil Defence, it is recorded the reason was to try and arrange for air raid shelters to be placed in the schools. They had been having lunch in the hotel at the time of the bombing, and Howard Sikes, the Senior Regional Technical Advisor from the Ministry of Home Security, was one of those killed.

Several of those who died were married couples. These included Raymond and Maud Bircham, who were in the Royal Observer Corps and the Women's Voluntary Service. Lt. Leonard R.E. Crute (aged 25 years) who was serving in the Royal Artillery and his wife Jean Crute (aged 22 years); Cpl. Wilfred John Peregrine (aged 32 years) who was serving in the Royal Air Force and his wife Mamie Dorothy Peregrine, an Air Raid Warden (aged 27 years).

Leonard and Jean Crute were staying at the Central Hotel with Jean's parents, Mr and Mrs Badcock. Mabel Badcock was with her daughter and son-in-law when the bomb struck. Leonard died instantly, but his wife Jean survived for a short period and was able to talk to her mother. Unfortunately Jean died before she could be rescued. It was 19 hours before Mabel was dug out alive. However she never recovered from the experience and died two years later aged 58 years. Mabel's husband Reginald, was on the ground floor at the time of the bombing and walked out of the rubble unharmed.

A young couple having a clandestine wartime assignation died together at the Central Hotel. It took months to identify their bodies and formal identification was eventually confirmed following an exhumation.

The bomb also caused major damage to the Punshon Memorial Church next door. Part of the spire toppled with the explosion. The roof and south wall were badly damaged, and the building was later demolished.

The Metropole Hotel in the Lansdowne was being used as a billet for the Air Force at the time and was packed full of servicemen. It had approximately 120 bedrooms spread out over 5 floors, with the bars and reception rooms on the ground floor, and other services in the basement. This imposing Victorian building built between 1891 and 1893 on the site of the Old Lansdowne House, was also a very popular meeting place for the local men. When the building was requisitioned, Mr Wilson, the manager, continued to hold an alcohol licence so the bar could remain open.

After the raid The Metropole Hotel, viewed from the Christchurch Road side, appeared almost untouched. However the bomb had penetrated the Holdenhurst Road side and this was devastated. The bomb had entered on the second or third floor, gone right through the building, then had exploded on contact with the steel and concrete staircase. The whole facia on the Holdenhurst Road side had been blown out in places, the result being the roof caved in and the floors and stairway collapsed. The damage has been described as though a giant hand had taken hold of the roof, lifted the building up, and then let go. The bodies of 11 civilians were recovered here, as were the bodies of the Canadian Airmen. The Home Office report gives the number of fatalities here as being 37, but once again the true number of deaths may never be known.

So severe was the explosion that some of the bodies were blown clear of the building. It was said that more than a week later an airmen's body was recovered from the College clock tower. It was only found because somebody went to investigate why all the seagulls were gathering around the tower. Some men were blown to bits in the cellar which was littered with body parts. Many of these would have been unidentifiable.

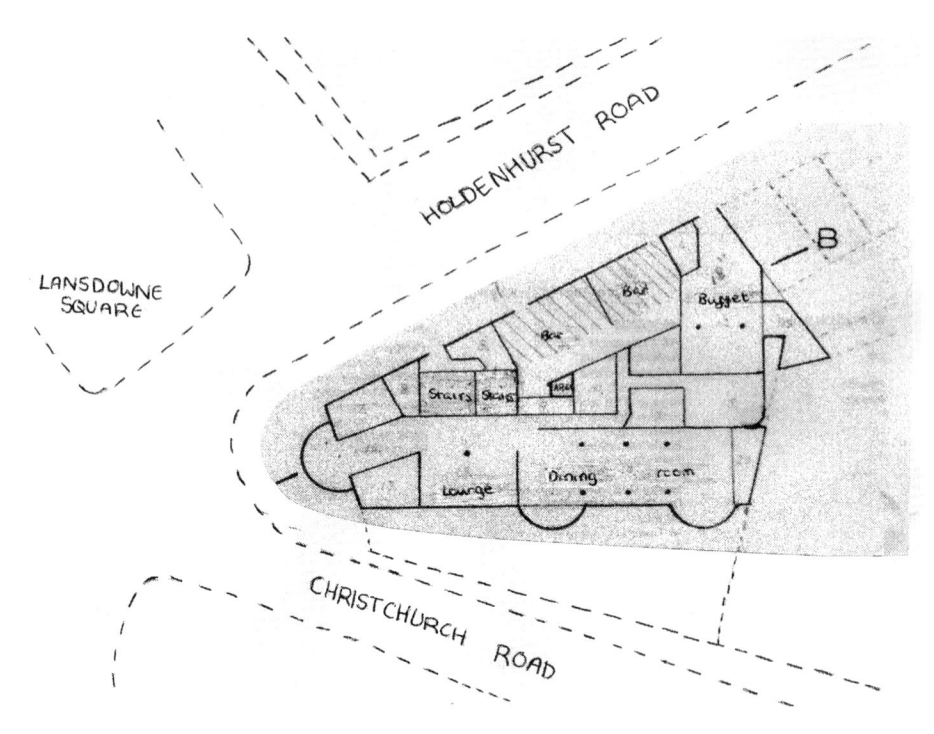

Ground Floor plan of The Metropole Hotel

The Metropole Hotel after the raid
pictured from Old Christchurch Road

The Metropole Hotel after the raid
pictured from Holdenhurst Road

WVS Canteen outside The Metropole Hotel

David Gear (left)

Merryweather Fire Engine with 100ft. turntable ladder

There was also heavy machine gunning in the area and some may have died looking out the windows, watching the aircraft as they flew past.

Harry Mears made the following entry in his memoirs: -

> *I then proceeded to the Lansdowne and arrived at the scene of the Metropole, here furious activity was going on as more and more rescuers burrowed into the mass of debris. The casualties here were very heavy and most of them were dominion airmen. The sight saddened me as I saw body after body dragged from the wrecked hotel, all young men who had been in the prime of life, cut down in seconds by the explosion of the bomb.*

There were many acts of bravery that day, but one of the most notable was that of Mr. David Gear, the Boiler-room Stoker at the Metropole Hotel. Mr. Gear was 76 years old at the time of the raid. He had previously worked at the hotel for 25 years prior to his retirement, but had returned to work for the duration of the war, being employed by the War Ministry. Mr. Gear escaped from the building, but returned to extinguish the boilers and turn off the gas supply, thereby ensuring fire did not break out.

His son John described the events as follows: –

> *On the Sunday when the Hotel was bombed, my father "Pop" to the family, was at work in the hotel boiler-room. My mother heard of the bombing that had taken place at the Lansdowne, and as I was home on leave from the Royal Navy, asked me to cycle to the hotel. I was in uniform and*

she thought I would have more chance of getting through the Police cordon, to see if "Pop" was safe. When I arrived there the Police informed me my father was okay and was making his way up the coal chute, onto the pavement. "Pop" was fine, but covered in soot, grime and debris. "Pop" then went back into the boiler room and turned off the boilers and gas supply, thus avoiding more devastation. "Pop" took all this in his stride and did not make a fuss. We left the area making our way home to Seafield Road, stopping off at the Pinecliffe Hotel at Fisherman's Walk, for a beer before we returned home.

For this feat of outstanding bravery Harry Mears recommended him for a gallantry award and he was later awarded a Certificate by the Kings Order from Winston Churchill and was Mentioned in Dispatches in the *London Gazette* on the 19th December 1944 for brave conduct in Civil Defence.

Mr. Gear was also awarded the "Three Silver Oak Leaves" by The Commander of the Canadian Air Force, based in Bournemouth.

After this episode, Mr. Gear did not work again, so saddened was he by the loss of "his dear boys", as he called the Canadian Air Force men who died that day. He retired on a pension of 10 shillings a week (50 pence in modern currency) and died in 1957 at the ripe old age of 91 years.

There were also incredible tales of people being blown clear by the blast and having recovered from the shock, found themselves on the other side of the road uninjured.

Bob Judd aged 22 years, had just come off guard duty and was on the third floor of the hotel having a bath at the time of the raid. When the walls blew in he was covered in glass and debris. He hastily found his clothes and identity disc then waited to be rescued by the Fire Brigade.

The Fire Service rescued 36 people from the Metropole Hotel, using their Merryweather 100ft. turntable ladder that had been acquired in June 1939. This was manned by 6 firemen, namely Roger Dehon and his crew of Leading Fireman Griffiths (a local school teacher), and Firemen Miles, Northover, Smith and Pearce,

Legend has it that a young airman had just gone to answer a call of nature when the bomb struck. He found himself in the embarrassing position of being seated on the lavatory with his trousers round his ankles. He was suspended in thin air, open to the elements, with only the soil pipe holding him up. All the walls and floors having been blown out, here he waited until he was rescued. A tribute to the strength of the Victorian plumbing.

Eddie Robichaud, a Canadian airman who was aged 21 at the time, recalled for Ted Hughes in his book *Bournemouth Firemen at War*: -

> *I'd gone up to see one of the corporals on the fourth floor at lunchtime. That was when the first bomb hit. Everything went dusty, then the second bomb hit and blew shut the*

door of the bedroom we were in. We waited for the dust to settle and saw the window had been blown out and was blocked up with bricks. I looked up at the wall and could see bodies crunched up in the chimney. We just kept shouting for a while and they got us out at about 4 o'clock.

Note: Firemen had to dig away the floor to rescue them.

The lives of many of the bar staff were also saved by a strong metal beam that had been inserted in the building to support an extension added a few years earlier. This ran above the main bar and took the weight of the blast in this area. Unfortunately one of the barmaids was said to have been beheaded.

Ruby Hudd, the young receptionist had been sent down to the cellar for a bottle of liquor moments before the bomb exploded. This probably saved her life. Her recollection of events that day can be found in the chapter Reports and Reminiscences.

Previously it was presumed that the majority of the Dominion Airmen died here. Official records confirm the Canadian Airmen as having died at the Metropole Hotel, but the Australians were killed at the Central Hotel.

The Metropole Hotel, previously known as the Palace Hotel, was owned by Levy and Franks, and managed at the time by Mr. N. R. Wilson. He had been appointed in 1934 to revive the fortunes of this establishment which had suffered during the slump and declined badly. This he did and within two years it had become one of the leading hotels on the south coast. The hotel had also been the family's first home. Mr Wilson subsequently became the manager of the Carlton Hotel.

At the outbreak of war, Sir Isadore Salmon, who was director of J. Lyons and Co., of Lyons Corner House fame, was appointed to advise on and oversee, all of the Royal Air Force catering arrangements. The responsibility for the catering arrangements of all the Dominion Air Force personnel that entered the country was delegated to Mr. Wilson. His duties included the requisitioning of buildings and hotels throughout the country, to accommodate the hundreds of thousands of men who entered via the liners, now turned troop ships. For security reasons they were given very little advance warning as to when or where the ships were docking, and accommodation for thousands of men had to be provided at very short notice, initially often only allowing 9 to 10 days for requisitioning the required buildings.

In all they provided hospitality for about 2 million service personnel. Mr. Wilson was presented to the King and Queen for his outstanding work, but refused any other recognition.

At the time of the raid, Mr Wilson and his family were living in Thistlebarrow Road, in Queen's Park. When Mr Wilson did not arrive home after the raid, Mrs Wilson became concerned and asked her son Jim, then aged 15 to cycle into town to see if he was safe. He was shocked at the grim sight that greeted him at the Metropole. However he soon located his father who was covered from head to foot in white dust but unhurt. Jim was familiar with the building's layout, having lived and played there as a child, and was soon asked to assist the rescue services to navigate their way around the cellars in their attempts to find and recover the dead and injured. His lasting memory is the sight of the covered bodies laid out, with their identification toe tags attached. Stoically, after helping out he returned home to reassure his mother.

The Bournemouth based No. 3 Personnel Reception Centre (3PRC) effectively turned the town into the largest Military unit in the U.K., its Headquarters being in the Royal Bath Hotel. An example of the unit's strength can be seen in the intake figures for the days following the raid. On Monday 24th May, and Tuesday the 25th, the intake comprised of the following:

24th May

96 Officer Pilots, 48 Observers, 7 Officer Air Bombers,
7 Officer WOP/AG's, 164 Sgt. Pilots, 84 Sgt. Observers,
21 Air Bombers, 178 Sgt. WOP/AG's, 18 Sgt. Air Gunners and 1,531 Airmen other trades.

25th May

16 Officer Observers, 19 Officer Air Bombers,
19 Officer WOP/AG's, 5 Officer Ground Trades
And 1 Airman Ground Trade.

The Commanding Officer heading the Dominion Airmen, was Group Captain Hutchinson, OBE, who was a Canadian from Alberta. He had only just assumed command of what was then called R.A.F. Station Bournemouth, from Group Captain O'Brian on the 8th of May.

Group Capt. G. S. O'Brian had flown with the Royal Flying Corps in the First Word War where he was awarded the AFC. He joined the R.C.A.F. in Toronto in 1932, and was on the reserve list in 1935. At the outbreak of war he joined up again on 3rd September 1939. On 1st January 1946, O'Brian by then an Air Commodore, was made CBE for his work in Bournemouth. The citation states that the average strength of the unit was 1,170 officers, 5,000 airmen, and 1,000 airwomen.

Bournemouth was also the centre for No. 11 Australian Personnel Dispatch and Receiving Centre (11 PDRC).

Lorries were brought in from all the surrounding areas to help move the dead and injured. The bodies were taken to two mortuaries. The first was in Littledown Road (East Yard). This was manned by Mr. T.M. Bailey, the Corporation Permanent Mortuary Superintendent, the other was an emergency mortuary set up at Iford in the old stabling, a single storey red brick building, adjacent to Castle Lane and Sheep Wash. This was manned by Deric Scott the undertaker who acted as Voluntary Emergency Mortuary Superintendent to oversee the proceedings. They received bodies from the hotels throughout the night. The rescue teams continued the body search for many days.

One of those helping with the rescue work at the Metropole Hotel, was Mrs. Betty Hockey. In the evenings Betty held concert parties to entertain the servicemen. However during the day she assisted the War Effort by collecting old tyres in her small van for salvage, for this she would have received a small petrol allowance. This meant she had one of the few vehicles on the road in the town at that time, transport that would have been very useful in helping moving the dead and injured.

Jack Hopkins

Another rescuer who arrived to help at The Metropole was a young Post Office engineer by the name of Jack Hopkins. He helped dig out the dead and injured and finally left at around 7 p.m. that night. He recalled how doctors had been brought to the scene to aid the injured young airmen, many of whom lost limbs having been trapped under the falling masonry.

It might be of interest to note here that the W.V.S. set up several mobile canteens to supply snacks and drinks to the rescue teams, and the Women's Service Club provided over 2,000 hot meals.

There were however more cheerful tales of recovery. A bus conductor was dug out of the rubble alive complete with his bicycle and attaché case, after the explosion in one of the hotels. He was cycling to work when the bomb blast hit him and he was buried. A Scottie dog was also recovered from the debris two and a half days after the explosion and lived to tell the tale.

More eyewitness and newspaper reports can be read in Reports & Reminiscences.

It is recorded that the area around the Gardens was heavily machine gunned. At the time, the press reports denied that there had been any deaths due to machine gunning, this would have been done to prevent panic amongst the general public. However two civilians are recorded as having died in the Gardens, these were Robert Robshaw (aged 37), and Abraham (Albert) Spinak, a musician aged 41 years.

The "clear up" operation was enormous, both in terms of structural damage to the town, and the loss of human life.

Acres of glass had been blown out in the town centre alone. This made the rescue operation hazardous in itself. There was the debris from the damaged and burnt out buildings and vehicles to remove. Reports of unexploded bombs across the town had to be investigated. Many of these turned out to be false alarms, the bombs just being the fins that had fallen off the bombs prior to them exploding. A consequence of very low level bombing.

Roads had to be made clear for traffic to use once again. Even with teams of workmen brought in from outside areas, this took days to complete. It was a week before the trolleybuses could once again use Richmond Hill and it was the end of August before traffic returned to normal in The Square, due to the damage to Bobby's. The roads around the remains of Beales did not reopen to traffic until the end of September.

Shelter and billets had to be found for those who had been bombed out. Businesses had to salvage what stock they could and find other premises to trade from.
In terms of human life, the hospitals had to deal with the hundreds of casualties, many of whom had very serious wounds, including amputations. Some needed weeks if not months of hospitalisation, before being allowed to convalesce. This would have required additional hospital beds and nursing staff to look after them.

The Royal Victoria Hospital in Boscombe was the main hospital for the Bournemouth area. It was only a small hospital at the time and although many of the injured were treated here, some would have been taken to neighbouring hospitals. Cornella Hospital in Poole (it was not known as Poole General Hospital until the N.H.S. was formed in 1948) was another major hospital and some of the casualties may have been taken there for treatment. There was a military hospital at Lilliput, and in 1943 U.S. Military Hospitals were established at Kingston Lacy, St. Leonard's, and Blandford.

The dead had to be identified and buried. The bodies were initially taken to the temporary mortuaries, before being removed by the undertakers or Military. It took months before some of the corpses could be formally identified; one Airman was buried as "unknown".

There were only a few undertakers in the town at that time, all working at full stretch. The family firm of George Scott and Son, had been awarded the Military contract. They handled the remains of 33 service men over the following days. Harold Scott the proprietor, despite being in a reserved occupation, was serving in the R.A.F. He had entered the service in October 1942, where his administrative skills were put to good use. The business was being run by his wife Lettice Scott and his sister Kathleen Paris, known in the family as "Aunty Kath". The only help they had was that of an elderly coffin maker. It is thought that Harold Scott had been stationed locally at the time of the raid and had been recalled home that week to help cope with the military funerals. They dealt with the remains of all the R.A.F., Canadian and Australian Airmen recovered from the town. Some of the bodies had suffered severe blast injuries and were almost unidentifiable.

The men were placed in elm coffins, with brass fittings, ready for burial. The remuneration for this arduous task was £5. 5s. 0d. (5 Guineas) per body; this was half the cost of some of the private funerals carried out by other undertakers. The bodies of the Canadian Airmen together with the German, were released on May 25th, the Australians on the 26th, and the Royal Air Force, on the 29th.

The coffined remains of some of the civilians and the military were returned to their home towns for burial. However places had to be found in the local cemeteries for the remainder and well over 100 graves duly dug.

Initially a mass grave was prepared; however this was not acceptable to some of the families and was never used. It was decided therefore to bury all the bodies individually, including the servicemen. It takes between four to six hours to dig an individual grave, depending on soil conditions, so this in itself was a massive undertaking in terms of man hours, considering how many bodies they had to bury in the short space of time.

The funerals of all the airmen who were buried in Bournemouth took place on the afternoon of Saturday 29th May. There were three half hour services commencing at 2.30 p.m. Also buried that day were members of the

Rescue Services who were killed in the line of duty, and some of the hotel workers.

The military graves can all be found in the North Cemetery, Strouden Avenue. These are maintained by The War Graves Commission.

There is no known memorial in the town dedicated to those who died that day. It is said that in 1944 the Officers of the Royal Canadian Air Force and the U.S.A.A.F. placed a set of three stained glass windows in one of the hotels then in use as an Officers Mess, as a tribute to the men that died. However no trace of the windows can be found today.

"THE FEW"

The gratitude of every home in our island, in our Empire, and indeed throughout the world, except in the abodes of the guilty, goes out to the British Airmen who, undaunted by odds, unwearied in their constant challenge and mortal danger, are turning the tide of the world war by their prowess and by their devotion. Never in the field of human conflict was so much owed by so many to so few.

Winston Churchill - Paying tribute to the Royal Air Force, House of Commons, 20th August 1940. This speech was made following his visit to Fighter Command Airfields in the South of England.

Canada is the linchpin of the English speaking world, Canada, with those relations of friendly, affectionate intimacy with the United States of America on the one hand and with her unswerving fidelity to the British Commonwealth and the Motherland on the other, is the link which joins together these great branches of the human family, a link which, spanning the oceans brings the continents into their true relation and will prevent in further generations any growth of division between the proud and the happy nations of Europe and the great countries which have come into existence in the New World.

Winston Churchill – Mansion House, London 4th September 1941, at a luncheon in honour of Mackenzie King, P.M. of Canada.

THE CONCLUSION

The question "Why Bournemouth?" has been asked for many years. The answer may lay in a comment repeated by young airmen from all over the world, "that if Hitler wanted to stop the war effort, all he had to do was bomb Bournemouth". This he did on May 23rd 1943. One young Airman from Australia wrote in his diary on Thursday 12th February 1942, following an Air Raid on Poole.

> *It is a wonder to me. As it is to all of us, why Bournemouth hasn't been blitzed. It certainly is a legitimate military objective, packed with soldiers and airmen, as it is. A few bombs to wipe out these hotels we are billeted in would be a real blow - would undo lots of time and work that has gone into the Empire Air Scheme.*

As said previously, the town was one of the main reception and training areas for the young Air Force crews who had come in from countries as far afield as Canada, Australia and New Zealand. Many of these men had crossed the Atlantic in the large liners such as the Queen Mary and Queen Elizabeth, before alighting at the ports of Southampton and Liverpool.

These luxurious vessels had been stripped of their fittings and converted into troop ships to carry the many men required to fight the war. It would not have been a luxury crossing, often 18 or 20 men shared a state room, sleeping in bunks. During the Second World War the Queen Mary carried more than 750,000 troops across the Atlantic. In July

1943 she carried on board 16,683 people, mostly troops, in a single voyage.

Bournemouth was not only a reception and training area, it was also a main rest and recreation centre for men, some of whom were suffering from battle fatigue or recovering from injuries.

Due to the number of different units in the town, the true number of military deaths that day may never be known. There were around 70 hotels in military use at that time, and many other buildings had been requisitioned. The town was packed full of servicemen and women of all units and nationalities. German intelligence would have been well aware of this. For many years there were rumours of a "spy" in Bournemouth, and there are indications that this might well have been the case.

The raid took place at a time when the war was at its height. Exactly a week previously, Bomber Command had carried out the famous "Dam Busters Raid" and on the night of 23rd/24th May 1943, 826 aircraft from Bomber Command bombed Dortmund in the Ruhr Valley. In this raid, many of the German factories were hit including the Hoesch Steel works, which ceased production. 38 aircraft failed to return from this mission. Three of the Canadian Airmen who died in the raid on Bournemouth, were with 408 Squadron (Goose Squadron). This was part of No.6 (R.C.A.F.) Group, who took part in the raid on Dortmund that night, some of whom did not return.

Flight Sergeants Abbott, Assaf and Soos were on leave here in the town. It was a popular leave centre. Many of the men had spent time in Bournemouth when they first arrived in the country and they felt relaxed here. The town was still full of Canadians, so they could be with their own countrymen, also "the locals were friendly", and compared to much of the rest of England, the weather was comparatively good. The Metropole was a large hotel, and a regular leave destination with the Canadian Servicemen.

It should be noted here that 55,573 men died from Bomber Command alone in World War II. A great number of the Air Crew would have spent time in the town, some only staying three or four days before joining their units.

Numerous notable events occurred in the town throughout the wartime period. It was at a meeting of the Labour Party's National Executive committee in one of the hotels (The Highcliff) in May 1940, that Clement Attlee their leader telephoned Downing Street, and announced that they would join a National Government, but only if Chamberlain withdrew as Prime Minister. Within 2 hours, King George VI asked Winston Churchill to form a Government.

On 21st October 1941, the King and Queen received Dominion Airmen at the Pavilion. In February 1944 Generals Eisenhower and Montgomery met at the Carlton Hotel, in preparation for the D-Day Landings. It has been said that they watched the rehearsals for the landings from the gardens of the Royal Bath Hotel.

It is well established that the American forces were present in the area at the time of the Raid. In 1942 Operation Bolero commenced. This was a massive movement of the U.S. Ground forces to Britain, in preparation for the opening of the second front in North West Europe. Bournemouth with all its hotels and amenities, became the ideal rest centre for American forces. From this date American accommodation was provided within the town and The Carlton Hotel had become the British Headquarters for The Military Branch of the F.B.I.

From the time it arrived, the 8th Airborne Division used the town for recreation and for post-battle rehabilitation. From America's entrance into the war in 1942, there had been a noticeable presence of U.S. forces at Hurn. German intelligence was well aware of its significance, for the newly constructed airfield was first bombed as early as December 1941.

The initial cadre of the American Ninth Air Force relocated to England from North Africa in May 1943. However they only became a significant presence in Bournemouth later that year when several of the New Forest airfields were handed over to them. Five advanced landing grounds were laid out for their use by R.A.F. Construction units in advance of the forthcoming D-Day invasion. Two new runways were constructed at R.A.F. Winkton to take three squadrons of Thunderbolts, other local airfields such as

Christchurch, Holmsley and Talbot Village, were extended to accommodate them. These men socialised in the American Red Cross hostels in the town, the Ambassador and Marsham Court Hotels had been requisitioned for this purpose and were very popular with the American Service personnel.

Several of the larger hotels were requisitioned for use as Officers Clubs, leave centres and by the American Red Cross. By the end of the war, 30 hotels were in use (or had been) by the American forces. In 1943 there were three U.S. Military Hospitals in the area. Kingston Lacy, which was mainly a convalescent centre, used by the 106th, St. Leonards (104th) and Blandford (22nd).

It is therefore logical that American Service personnel would be amongst the casualties. Contemporary newspaper reports stated that Canadian, Australian and U.S. visitors were among the voluntary helpers that assisted with the clear up. One photograph shows an American Army lorry outside the damaged Metropole Hotel.

It is now known that 6 men from the U.S 175th Infantry Regiment, 29th Division, died in the air raid (details shown in Military Dead). They were on leave from Tidworth. The casualties are recorded in the book *29 Let's Go!, A history of the 29th Division in World War II*, as being the first men in the division to die as a result of enemy action.

Clearing debris at The Metropole Hotel
(Note: American Army lorry in foreground)

The Division arrived in England on board the Queen Mary on 5th October 1942. In May 1943 the Division moved to Devon and Cornwall where it conducted simulated attacks on fortified positions. At this time it was assigned to V Corps of the U.S. Army.

The bodies of those killed in Bournemouth were initially taken to Brookwood Cemetery. Three were then taken to the American Military Cemetery at Madingley. It must be assumed that the families of the others chose to have their bodies repatriated.

Another small but significant fact that may have had an influence on the date of the raid, was that the Bournemouth Municipal Orchestra was celebrating its 50th Anniversary that day. Two concerts had been planned at the Winter Gardens, one in the afternoon and the other in the evening. *The Times* newspaper reported in its edition on May 21st, that the programme would be broadcast on the radio from 6.45 – 7.30 p.m. It would have been quite a propaganda coup for the Germans had this concert been cancelled. The concerts both went ahead, with nearly two thousand people attending. Sir Adrian Bolt and Montague Birch both conducted the afternoon concert, where Elgar's "Nimrod" from the Enigma Variations was played as a tribute to those who had died. Montague Birch conducted the evening concert that was broadcast. The atmosphere at the concerts that day were not surprisingly described as "chill and dreary".

In conclusion this appears to have been an intelligence based strategic raid by the Germans in an attempt to reduce the effects the allied airmen were having on the German war machine.

THE COMBATANTS
AND TECHNICAL SPECIFICATIONS
OF AIRCRAFT

Background of IV/SKG/10

SKG10 was formed by combining the specialist fighter bomber Staffeln and Gruppes from several fighter Geschwader on the channel coast, into a fast bomber Geschwader. It included pilots from 10/JG2, one of the most successful fighter bomber units against British coastal shipping in the Channel area. IV/SKG/10 had only been formed a month and comprised of men with varying experiences, all of whom had shown a particular aptitude to fast low level bombing.

At the time of the raid it was based in Carpiquet Aerodrome, Caen, in Northern France. However in June - August of that year it moved to the Mediterranean to thwart the Allied invasion of Sicily. After the invasion the unit was then moved to the Eastern Front in Russia and became 11/SG/10.

Of the 26 men that carried out the raid on Bournemouth, the following details are known.

Uffz. Rudi Agethen: Died 6th March 1945

Uffz . Helmut Bachle:

Uffz. Klaus Gehrke:

Uffz. Bernd Hofmeister: Died 23rd April 1944

Uffz. Herbert Kanngeter: Taken prisoner of war 30th May 1943

Gefr. Karl Laue: Died 30th May 1943

Lt. Werner Margarin: (Flight Sergeant) Died 27th Dec. 1943. Shot down over Russia.

Ofw. Max Meixner: Died 21st August 1944

Uffz .Hans Muller:

Lt. Erhard Nippa: Born 7th Feb. 1922 in Danzig-Langfuhr. Entered the war in 1942 first serving with 10/JG2 (Richthofen), then went to IV/SKG/10. On leaving IV/SKG/10, he served with 11/SG/10. He flew BF 109F-4, and FW190A aircraft.

He was awarded the following: - DK.G (29.04.43) RK (26.03.44) EK1+2 Assault Op. clasp w/300 (awarded for having flown 300 missions). The RK having been awarded for his fighter/bomber and close support sorties on both ground and shipping targets.
He is recorded as having sunk both a Destroyer and a Freighter.
Died 27th June 2003.

Uffz. Ostermann:

Uffz. Fredrich Karl Schmidt: Born Herne, Westf. 19th Jan. 1922.

Identity Disc: 3/Fl.A.R.32/809

Died 23rd May 1943.

Shot down during the raid on Bournemouth by gunners on the roof of the East Cliff Court Hotel. His aircraft crash landed on to the flat roof of The St. Ives Hotel, 34 Grove Road. He was dead on impact.

This was his first operational flight. Part of his diary was recovered from the crash. A translation of which, can be seen below.** These details have been taken from the "Secret" A.I.(K) Report No, 237/1943 made at the time of his crash. The document was signed by Wing Commander S.D. Felkin and is dated 26th May 1943.

Uffz. Eugen Streich: Born 7th Feb. 1920 in Ebingen.

Served with 15/SKG/10 flew FW190A-5/U8.

Died of injuries sustained on landing when returning from the raid on Bournemouth 23rd May 1943. During the raid an aircraft was damaged and was seen exiting low over Bournemouth Bay. This may well have been Streich, for he struck a tree with the starboard wing on landing, which was ripped off, causing the aircraft to cartwheel across the field.

Uffz. Streich was taken to the Luftwaffe hospital at Caen, but died of his injuries.

Uffz. Eugen Streich

Eugen Streich's decorated grave

Uffz. Eugen Streich's funeral, Caen 1943

<u>Oblt. Leopold "Poldi" Wenger:</u> Born Graz Austria 11/19/1921.

Officially flew 372 missions (71 Fighter bomber missions), but is known to have flown over 450.

Served in the following units- 3/JG2, 10(Jabo) JG2, STFKPT, IV/SKG/10, STFKPT 4/SG-10, STFKPT 6/59-103.

Leopold Wenger flew FW190A and FW190F-8 aircraft, and is recorded as having shot down at least five planes.

On returning to France from a raid, he and another pilot were pursued across the Channel by two spitfires. One was piloted by a Canadian named Barry Needham, who fired at Wenger, damaging his hydraulics. However he landed without difficulties in France.

Oblt. L. Wenger held the following honours:-
RK(14/1/45)DK-9,EK 1+2, Assault Op Group Clasp W/"300" Hanger.

He was killed in action on 10.4.1945 in Deutsch-Wagram, by a Soviet Yak.

Buried Vienna XX11 Hirschstetten.

**   <u>The Diary of Friedrich Schmidt</u>

1943

1st -2nd **Jan.**	in Cambrai.
5th	in Antwerp.
9th	Laon.
16th	Lt. Mertens crashes near Rebbel –Killed.
18th	Force landing in Comines.
20th	Lt. Daziers body recovered.

22nd	Another aircraft crashes. Pilot dead. Gefreiter Siegel force lands, unhurt.
23rd	Short flight in Arado Ar 96.
25th	Burial of ………………..
26th	A Feldwebel and a Unteroffizier crash. Both killed.
27th	Flight.
1st-28th **Feb**	Ten practice flights with the Me 109D &E also bombing and firing practice.
2nd **March**	Firing practice. Landed safely in bad weather with the Me 109D. Got down safely.
5th	Braun crashes in Me 109E at take off.
6th	Bombing Practice.
13th	Go on leave.
3rd **April**	Leave ends.
5th	Leave Berlin 2245 hours Anhaelter.
6th	Arrive Paris East at 2045 hours. Leave Paris/Austerlitz 2300 hours.
7th	Arrive Bordeaux 0700 hours. Arrive Cognac 1900 hours.
13th	First flight out to sea.
17th	Hauptmann Kellenberger in the drink. One wheel and a cushion recovered.
20th	New Schwarm leaders arrive, including Oberfeldwebel Peterbusch. 15 victories, holder of the Ritterkreuz. (Knights Cross).
23rd	Touching down, left tyre bursts – 15% damage.

24th	Saecki buried.
27th	Daily practice flights.
28th	Bernd crashes, 85% damage. Uninjured.
30th	Hauptmann Kellenberger washed up.
3rd **May**	Go to Royan
	Hauptmann Kellenberger buried.
4th	Escort "Sperrbrecher 5" from Royan to La Rochelle. Explode three mines. Brought out an Italian U-Boat.
7th	Leave Cognac.
8th	Posted to Caen.
10th	Arrived Caen – 15th Staffel.
11th	Flight with Staffelkapitaen.
12th	Flight.
14th	Put a FW 190 on its nose.
15th	Battle HQ. Inauguration ceremony. Tommy makes his first Attack.
17th	Pamphlets – (apparently an R.A.F. nickel raid in the vicinity).
18th	The castle is officially opened.
19th	Bernd force lands on the airfield. No damage.
22nd	Tommy delivers a night attack.

On the back of the diary, barely decipherable, were the following notes-

19.11.39	Fl.Aus.Reg. 32, 3 Komp., Uetersen
5.1.40	Sch. Fl. Aus. Regt. 32, Pardubitz

6.3.40	Flg. H. Kp., Finsterwalde
28.4.40	------------E.27/?
14.8.40	Sch. Fl. Aus. Rgt. 53, Heiligenbeil
1.2.41	F.F.S. A/B 123, Agram
19.4.41	Jagdvorschule 1, Kamenz
8.12.41	" "
6.1 .42	4.F.F.S. A/B 120, Prenzlau
16.6.42	Zerstorarvorschule (Nancy)
14.10.42	Schlachtfliegerschule, Reims
4. 4.43	Ersatzschnellkampfverband, Cognac
15.5.43	15: S.K.G. 10, Caen.

Translation of Friedrich Schmidt's diary courtesy Aircrew Remembrance Society.

THE SQUADRONS OF R.A.F. IBSLEY
MAY 1943

There were three squadrons based in Ibsley in May 1943.

1. **129 (Mysore) Squadron.**
Code: DV e.g. DV-V serial EE602.
Arrived Ibsley 13th March 1943 (second tour).
Departed 28th June for Hornchurch.
They flew the Spitfire Mk. Vb

2. **504 (County of Nottingham) Squadron.**
Code TM e.g. TM-R serial EE624.
Arrived Ibsley 30th December 1942 from Middle Wallop.
Departed 30th June 1943 for Church Stanton.
They flew Spitfires Mk.Vb and Vc.

3. **616 (South Yorkshire) Squadron.**
Code YQ e.g. YQ-A serial BS114.
Arrived Ibsley 18th March 1943 (second tour).
Departed June 17th for Exeter.
At Ibsley they flew Mk. V and VI Spitfire. (Note: on moving to Exeter these were replaced with the Mk. VII.).
As a result of their high level pressurised experience, 616 Squadron were the first and only allied squadron to fly jets in WW2, when they were equipped with the Meteor.

The Commanding Officer in May 1943 was S/Ldr. P. B. Lucas DFC.

In 1943 Spitfire Squadrons normally consisted of 16 aircraft, flying up to 12 on a mission. On combat missions, Ibsley generally flew with all three squadrons up. Due to the closure mechanism of the cockpits having to be sealed externally (to guarantee partial pressurisation), the Mk. VI Spitfire was not suitable for scramble. The records show the Wing had already been up twice that day, so a flight of four Spitfires as seen by Oblt. Wenger would equate to the "readiness flight" at Ibsley, getting away when the alert was raised by radar.

The Spitfire Vb and Vc were not fast enough to catch a FW190 in flight. The VI was even slower at low altitude and would not have been able to catch SKG/10 in a tail chase. At that time only the Typhoon would be capable of that.

In May 1943, 276 Squadron were based at Warmwell, on Air Sea Rescue, recovering men from the Channel. During this period they had two Spitfires that were used for fighter cover during rescue missions. These may well have been sent to Bournemouth and could explain the inconsistencies in the reports of events that day. Also operating from Warmwell at that time were 257(Jan-Aug '43) and 266 (Jan-Sept '43) Squadrons, both of which were flying Typhoons.

THE AIRCRAFT

At the time of the raid, the FW190 was a far superior aircraft to the Spitfire. It was more solidly built than the Messerschmitt 109, faster, due in part to its air cooled engine and could carry a heavier bomb load. It was capable of carrying a mixed pay load, often consisting of a 500kg bomb under the fuselage and four x 50 kg bombs under the wings. This was double the bomb load of the Me 109. However the pay load was often limited by fuel capacity.

Specifications of The Focke Wulf 190A-5

Manufacturer: Focke Wulf Flugzeugbau FmbH
Year: 1941
Engine: 1, BMW 801D-2, 14 cylinders, R, AC, 1700 hp
Wingspan: 34 ft 9in. (10.49 m)
Length: 29ft 4in. (8.94 m)
Height: 12ft 9in. (3.89 m)
Weight: 7,716 lbs, (3,499 kg)
Ceiling: 33,800 ft. (10,302 m)
Range: 495 miles (796 km)
Armament: 2x7.92 mm machine guns; 2x20mm cannon; 1,100 lbs of bombs.
Crew: One.

The Mark V Spitfire.

6,787 of these machines were built between August 1939 and October 1941.

Manufacturer: Supermarine
Engine: Rolls-Royce Merlin
Wingspan: 36 feet 10 inches
Length: 29 feet 11 inches
Weight: 5,065 lbs
Max. Power: 1,440-1,470 hp
Max speed: 371 mph at 20,000 feet.
Ceiling: 37,500 feet.
Fuel capacity: 87 Gallons.
In combat, a full tank may only last 30 mins.
Armament: Four .303 Browning Mk II machine guns and two 20 mm Hispano cannon
Crew: One

The Spitfire Mk VI

Only 97 of these high altitude aircraft were built. They had elongated wings and could fly at 39.000 feet. They were flown by some 13 squadrons, although only two squadrons 124 and 616 flew them exclusively. After this period, some of the aircraft had their wings clipped and their pressurised cabins removed so they could be used as training aircraft, although it is not thought this happened whilst they were based at Ibsley.

THE GERMAN STRATEGY AND PLAYERS

In "The Conclusion", it is surmised that the raid was an intelligence based response to the Allied bombing of German factories and towns on the Ruhr Valley. This theory is reinforced by research undertaken by W. Wenger, the brother of Leopold Wenger, who by studying controlled reports and letters, formed the opinion that the raid was ordered by the highest authority in the Luftwaffe, probably Hermann Goering personally.

It was said the attack was in reprisal to a heavy bombing raid by hundreds of Allied aircraft, in which over 1,000 civilians, mainly women and children were killed. It is believed that Generalmajor D. Peltz, one of the most experienced German bomber pilots and the youngest German general, was issued with the orders to plan out the strategy of the raid, with Major Heinz Schumann executing the final attack.

Two of Schumann's leading airmen were Erhard Nippa and Leopold "Poldi" Wenger. These men had served together in JG2, "The Red Foxes". This motif was chosen after Erhard Nippa at breakfast one morning in the mess, suggested it was time they had an emblem. Much discussion followed until they finally decided on a fox. For several days they tried to paint the design on paper without success. When they showed their efforts to the squadron commander, he was not impressed. Eventually

Hauptmann Frank Liesendahl asked his fiancée, Fraulein Arnold, a young designer with Messerschmitt, to design the emblem. This was used by the group throughout the war.

Erhard Nippa was the youngest of the comrades, having entered the war in 1942. He is described as being the friendly member of the group, always happy, always in a good mood, always the gentleman. He saw considerable combat experience and was awarded the Knights Cross on 26th March 1944. He later became a colonel in the new German Luftwaffe.

During the Munich Olympic Games in 1972, he had led the procession of the stewardesses. From this he developed a friendship with Sylvia, Queen of Sweden, who met her husband at the Olympics. Erhard Nippa died in 2003, and has been described by friends as "a great and wonderful man".

Erhard Nippa and Leopold Wenger remained the closest of friends for the three years they served together until Leopold's death in 1945.

Leopold Wenger, "Poldi" as he was known to his friends and family, was born in Graz in Austria in November 1921. He was the eldest of four children, the son of Leopold and Margarethe Wenger. His mother had been a primary school teacher at Bad Gleichenberg. His father had a love of the sea, and had served in the Royal Austrian Navy until

1918, when the Navy had been dispersed following the Versailles Treaty. In June 1911, at the age of 18, he had been on board the battleship "Radetzky" when it took part in the famous Spithead Review off Portsmouth, held to celebrate the coronation of King George V. Following the Navy's disbandment, he like many others, had to find other employment and eventually became the manager of a roofing company.

Leopold's siblings were Willy (born 1926), Gretel (born 1935) and Gerd (born 1939).

Poldi attended the Nationalpolitische Erziehungsanstalt, one of the elite schools of the "Drittes Reich". In 1938 on leaving school having finished his Matura (the equivalent of modern "A" levels), he went on to the military academy for Luftwaffe Officers. He left the academy in November 1939 when he was aged 18, and entered directly into the Luftwaffe to commence his training as a pilot.

In December 1940, on completion of his training, he received his first posting to the Jagdgeschader Richthofen JG2 at Le Havre, as a fighter pilot flying Me 109's. Whilst he was with them, he was part of the air escort for the battleships Scharnhorst, Gneisenau and Prinz Eugen when they entered the Channel waters. In 1942 he was posted to fighter bomber squadron (staffel) 10 of JG2, The Red Foxes. Here their main targets were shipping convoys, and the docks and ports along the English south coast.

Lt. Leopold "Poldi" Wenger

Lt. Leopold Wenger's FW. 190 in hanger

Jagdgeschader Richthofen JG 2, 9th July 1942
Left to Right: Oblt. Fritz Schroter, Lt. Gerhard Limberg, Lt. Leopold Wenger, Unknown (believed to be Obst. Karl Hentschell), Ofw. Werner Margarin, Hptm. Frank Liesendahl, Uffz. Kurt Bressler, Lt. Erhard Nippa

IV/SKG/10 prior to take off, May 23rd 1943
L to R: Klaus Gehrke, Max Meixner, Werner Margarin, Purps (ground crew)
Helmut Bachle, Karl Schmidt, Erhard Nippa,
Bernd Hofmeister, Eugen Streich, Rudi Agethen,
Kneeling/lying: Hans Muller, Karl Laue, Ostermann
Herbert Kanngeter (holding dog)

IV/SKG/10 prior to take off, May 23rd 1943

"The Blackmen" groundcrew at Caen - Carpiquet

"The Red Foxes"
Eckleben, Nippa, Wenger

"The Red Foxes" emblem

Throughout his service, he frequently wrote home to his family, although he was not allowed to reveal strategic or military details, nor to give the names of the men he was serving with. On the afternoon following the raid, he sent a letter home to his mother, in which he wrote: -

> *Today we flew a long range large scale attack. I led this mission and am the squadron leader. We attacked Bournemouth very effectively, a large number of bombs were dropped and considerable destruction caused. The English gunners engaged us and we replied with our own cannon. We were pursued by four Spitfires, but there was no air battle. This large scale attack has made a big impression on our young pilots, and has raised their enthusiasm for these missions considerably. Unfortunately we were not able to celebrate our success with cake and coffee because we are on standby; we will make up for it on an appropriate occasion.*
>
> *A short time ago a well known Major gave me a wonderful fur waistcoat as a gift. I will send it home as soon as possible.*

The major is thought to be Heinz Schuman.

At the time of the raid, it must be remembered that Poldi Wenger was only 21 years old, and yet he speaks about "our young pilots". He already held the position of *staffelführer* having been appointed on 10th April 1943 and a few days later he was to become the leader of 13/SKG10. He remained the squadron commander of the Red Foxes until 31st January 1945.

He was a quiet conscientious, ambitious man, who strove to achieve the best in whatever he did. His last log book held by the family ending in August 1944 shows he had flown 368 missions, however in a letter written to his parents in December 1944, he reveals he had flown more than 400 missions. They heard nothing more from him after February 1945, for all the mail had stopped, but it is known he flew over 450 missions.

The war had started to take its toll, many of the young officers found themselves in a moral conflict. The last time Willy met his brother Poldi at home, was at the end of 1943. They discussed the war, and Poldi said: -

> *What they had to do was terrible, it was a crime and he and his comrades were very afraid, that if they were captured by the British they would be tried like murderers.*

He also said that several of the pilots had lost family members in the R.A.F.'s night attacks on Germany.

This is reinforced by a conversation between Poldi's brother and Erhard Nippa in 1999, where Erhard Nippa confessed: -

> *Herr Wenger, every time I had to climb into that cockpit, it was agony.*

Right up until 1944 cadets at the Luftkriegsschule (the Luftwaffe Academy for Officers) were being taught to follow the Geneva Convention. However on the ground, politically based orders and the demands for revenge, over-rode the "rules" of war.

In June 1943, the Staffel moved to Sicily, where they attacked convoys and flew air to ground attacks on tanks etc. Here Poldi was wounded and spent several months in the Military Hospital in Germany. On recovery, he returned to his Staffel which had now moved to the Eastern Front in the Ukraine. Here he continued fighting air to ground attacks against Soviet tanks and installations in South Ukraine, Romania and Hungary.

In January 1945 he was awarded the Ritterkreuz. As usual after this, as one of the most experienced pilots, he became an instructor, training younger pilots. However at the beginning of April, Poldi returned to his Staffel, following the closure of the flying school.

There were times when Poldi seemed almost invincible. Several times his aircraft had suffered combat damage. One occasion his aircraft was shot full of holes, even his sun glasses had been shot away, yet he was uninjured. On another occasion he was fired at by Barry Needham, a Canadian pilot from Saskatchewan, whose ammunition penetrated Poldi's oil tank causing it to leak into the cockpit. Poldi told the family "he felt like a sardine in oil", he could not see anything. But he still managed to make his way back to the airfield in France. One of the mechanics repairing the aircraft, handed a shell to Poldi. This was kept by the family for more than 60 years, until September 2004, when Barry Needham visited Willy Wenger who presented it to him. Barry had been convinced he had killed Poldi, and that he had crashed into the Channel, and was very surprised to hear he had lived. At the time, he tried so hard to kill him, but years on he was very glad he had failed. If both men had survived the war, he is sure they would have been close friends, sharing their love of flying.

On 10th April 1945 (Poldi's father's birthday) Poldi took off from an airfield in Markersdorf in Austria, on an air to ground attack against Russian tanks near Vienna. It was to be his last mission. He was shot down over Vienna, managed to make an emergency landing, but his wounds were severe. He had lost too much blood and he never recovered. It was just 4 weeks before the end of the war. He was 23 years old.

It was originally thought he had been shot down by a Soviet Yak. However there was much discussion between members of his staffel who witnessed the event. They believe he was lured into a trap by the Russian Air Force, using a captured FW190, flown by either a Russian or Hungarian pilot.

Poldi's Katschmarek (wingman), a young pilot, recalled the following:-

On the way back from a mission on Russian tanks, they came across an air battle in the area of Ganserndorf near Vienna. Poldi ordered him to return to the base at Markersdorf, while he turned and flew towards the attacking fighters who came flying out of the sun. However an anti-aircraft gun came between.

It was sometime before the family were informed of his death. His brother Willy returned home at the end of June 1945, expecting Poldi to be there, however it was not until the November that they received any news. This came in the form of an official letter, dated and stamped 15th April, stating that he had been reported missing. The letter had been delayed due to the intervention of the Allied military censors. His family hoped he had been taken prisoner by the Russians, but in autumn 1948, more than three years after he had been reported missing, a letter was received from the Black Cross International informing the family that Poldi had been killed three and a half years earlier, and that he had been buried at the cemetery of Hirschstatten, near Vienna. In 1970 the bodies of all the military dead were exhumed and reburied at the Soldiers Cemetery in Vienna.

All Poldi ever wanted to do was fly. It was his passion, his life, and he died doing what he loved.

Only three officers from the original 10/Jagdeschwader Richthofen survived the war; Erhard Nippa, Gerhard Limberg and Fritz Schroter. Erhard Nippa died in 2003 and Fritz Schroter in 2007. Following the war, Gerhard Limberg became the highest commanding officer of the New Deutsche Luftwaffe Inspectorate. He was still alive in 2010, however he did not wish to discuss the war.

Young men are very inspired, and want to become fighters. Later when we are older, our views change and we can not understand why after all the miseries and bad experiences, nobody learns anything. W. Wenger 2010

The above section has been written using information supplied by Herr Wenger and Mrs Nippa from unpublished sources held within the families. The author wishes to express her gratitude for their understanding and assistance.

Translation from the German by Janina Bahm

REPORTS AND REMINISCENCES

From newspaper cuttings dated 24th May 1943

Large numbers of service men and civilians worked side by side with the Civil Defence and Fire Service personnel clearing rubble in order to reach the trapped people. They formed human chains across the road, passing the debris from hand to hand, so that the road soon became piled high with heaps of brick, mortar, woodwork and wrecked furniture.

....

HOTELIER RESCUED

Wearing blood-stained trousers, with his left arm in a sling, his eyes bandaged, and his cheek swollen, but still smoking a consoling cigarette, the landlord of the hotel said: "I was standing at the top of the front step when I heard the racket. I shouted 'duck' and ducked myself.

The explosion took place behind me and I got it on the back. It must have been half-an-hour before I 'came to', and I'm sure I owe my life to my having been standing outside the hotel.

"But where is my wife? That's what I want to know. I am waiting for my 'missus'."

"The hotel," he added, "was filled last evening, but a number of visitors went away on the early train to-day.

As for myself, I was lucky. I had chucked up the sponge, and then I saw a gleam of daylight through the muck under which I was buried. I found I could breathe and I attracted the rescuers to where I was. They tunnelled and found me."

....

An officer stated: "Men were clearing the rubble from one of the hotels when one of them said, 'There is a cavity here.' After an hours digging we recovered a bus conductor, his cycle and his attaché case. Apparently he was cycling to work when he was struck by bomb blast and buried. He suffered from injured feet."

Bournemouth Echo, May 25th 1943.

....

A visitor who showed remarkable courage and endurance was Mrs. Badcock, of Newton Abbot, who was buried in the ruins of a hotel. Rescue workers could hear her speaking cheerfully and doing her best to assist in directing operations.

They tunnelled from three different directions and extricated her after 19½ hours.

One of the rescue squad said, "She was very cheerful, and she gave us a smile when we brought her out. She is a very plucky woman."

Bournemouth Echo, May 24th 1943.

....

Search was also made among other extensively damaged buildings, but it is feared that many bodies may never be found.

Landmarks familiar to thousands of holidaymakers have disappeared. One departmental store was extensively damaged by fire. The flames spread to adjoining buildings, including shop, offices, a furniture store and a cinema. It took about four hours to get the fires under control.

Daily Telegraph, May 24th 1943.

....

A lovable little black Scottie dog was last night brought out by diggers from the debris of a hotel demolished in a raid on a south coast town on Sunday.

The dog had been buried for two and a half days but was unharmed and waddled joyfully away on its lead to a nearby canteen for a drink of milk.

"Is the 'Dumb Friends' League' man down there?" called a begrimed tin-hatted rescue worker in the light of the brilliant flares. "We've found a dog!"

The half-dozen or so watchers on the roadway then observed that the animal was lying like a baby across the chest of the rescuer, with its forepaws one on each side of his neck.

When Scottie was set upon his four legs he staggered backwards a little and seemed likely to fall, but recovered and gave himself a shake, setting up a miniature barrage of dust.

A police-officer deciphering with difficulty the name on the animal's identity label, said, "The owner was a victim."

Scottie ignorant of this gave a joyful little bark and shook itself again.

"I'll get him some milk," said a well known local colonel, as taking the animal's lead he went to an all-night canteen.

"Well that dog deserves a clap for his British spirit," said a Tommy, and the six or seven sturdy, tough men who had witnessed the incident joined in the applauding for a little black dog, as it receded into the night, for a much needed drink.

Bournemouth Echo, May 26th 1943.

……………………………………………

Picture if you can a road with blinding smoke along it, water being pumped into a blazing cinema and having found an outlet, is torrenting along the gutters. In two or three minutes your eyes begin to cloud over and smart – you cannot stand the smoke.

Yet standing on a perilously leaning heap of masonry is a W.A.A.F. corporal, helping to man a hose. Her eyes are bloodshot and tears have made tiny channels through the grime on her face. Here was news and I clambered over to her, but she could not give me her name. She was "only doing what any other girl in the unit would have done," she said.

Bournemouth Times, May 28th 1943.

……………………………………………

A pile of bricks and girders are all that remain of two houses and a furniture depository in one street. One bomb was responsible for all the damage.

In full view in front of the debris could be seen the roast dinner that had been cooking. It had been thrown out of the oven by the force of the explosion. A splash of colour was visible amongst the grey dirt rubble- painted cardboard boxes that once contained a child's toys. Carpets blown to the other side of the road hung on the tall trees like canopies.

Bournemouth Times, May 28th 1943.

....

At one of the hotels which had been hit and where people were still trapped, among the rescue parties was a strapping big fellow aged about 35. He bends down, grasps a huge chink of masonry, lifts it and dumps it on to a barrow, then repeats the process. I watched him for a short while and estimated that he would use more energy and shift more rubble in an hour than the average navvy would in a day.

His once khaki coloured trousers and shirt were coated with brick dust and a crash helmet finished his ensemble.

I was privileged to meet him in different circumstances recently, on which occasion he was immaculately dressed and the crown of a Major shone brightly on his shoulder.

Bournemouth Times, May 28th 1943.

....

I was a mere schoolboy in 1943 and when the air raid warning sounded I didn't take much notice as I was out in the garden at the time planting out some carrots for the night-fighters. Suddenly the roar of approaching planes came from the direction of the cliff top. I looked up and I could see a line of aircraft speeding towards me.

I ran an aeroplane spotters' club with a few school-friends, and immediately recognised the planes as Focke-Wulf fighter bombers. There were eighteen of them all together and they were firing off their machine guns at anything and everything as they sped over the town.

The town was full of men of the Royal Canadian Air Force and the Royal Australian Air Force as Bournemouth was a reception centre to which the gallant air men from the colonies came as soon as they arrived in Britain prior to posting to operational units. They occupied several of the larger hotels in town, notably the old Metropole Hotel at the Lansdowne, now Royal London House. This received a direct hit from a 500 pounder, and many Canadians were killed.

One body was recovered over a week after the raid from the clock tower of the Municipal College opposite the hotel – it had been blown up there by the freak blast. The same freak effect blew airmen out of the upper windows and actually cushioned them as they landed in front of the hotel. One of my school chums was near the Lansdowne at the time and saw an airman drop from an upper window. He brushed his tunic down and ran to the main entrance to help his comrades.

Of course, the Central Hotel on Richmond Hill was also hit, along with the old Punshon Memorial Church and Beales department store. I spent the afternoon helping to push a trolleybus in Old Christchurch Road as there was a danger from a burning building damaged by an incendiary bomb.

The Bournemouth Pleasure Gardens instantly became an open-air mortuary with what seemed like hundreds of bodies lying there covered with white cloths. The old bungalow at the end of Castle Lane near the Iford Roundabout was also used as a mortuary later that day. It was a red brick building at the time.

One of the Focke-Wulf fighter bombers was shot down and bits fell all around the Linden Hall Hotel area near the entrance to Boscombe Gardens. I remember I had a large piece of the rudder for years with a number and part of the swastika painted on it.

We used to listen to Lord Haw-Haw in those far-off days, and I tuned in to him that evening and heard him announce "Jar-minny calling, Jar-minny calling" (that was how he used to talk) . . . "Aircraft of the gallant Luftwaffe today attacked the busy port of Bournemouth on England's South Coast, and direct hits were scored on military installations."

By John Morley from *The Blitz Then & Now Vol. 3* by Winston G. Ramsey.

....

It was a beautiful warm sunny day and peacefully quiet. I was sat on the small balcony of the Vale Royal Hotel – I could look out to sea through a gap to my left. All of a sudden there was an ear-shattering roar of aircraft engines. I looked and saw a line of German Aircraft at roof top height. They immediately opened fire with cannon and released their bombs. I dived back into my room as cannon fire ripped into the hotel where the Bournemouth International Centre now stands. A bomb landed close to the Vale Royal which sent the hotel so far out of true that I expected the hotel to collapse. The raid was over in seconds – there had been no warning and the devastation was dreadful.

I lost many Canadian friends particularly in the Metropole Hotel where I had been billeted a few weeks before. Bud Abbott and I trained together – it was his habit to go to the gym and all that they found of his body was the torso. He could only be identified by his outstanding build. He was buried with many other in Bournemouth.

Cyril Alright - Taken from *Luftwaffe Fighter-Bombers over Britain* by Chris Goss

....

I had just sat down to lunch in the Osborne Hotel overlooking the Pleasure Gardens when the staccato rat-tat-tat of machine-gun fire flattened us to the floor. I glanced up through the window to see a Focke-Wulf pulling out of its dive over the Gardens. Then the window shattered and a stream of cannon shells embedded themselves along the wall of the dining room, when things quietened down then my first thoughts were to get back to HQ where my service would be urgently needed. As all the public transport was at a standstill, I had to make it across the town on foot, picking my way through masses of contents of shops littering the road when their windows had been blown out. As I approached the Lansdowne, the sight of what was left of the Metropole Hotel made my heart miss a beat, realising that some of my comrades were inside it. Then it suddenly dawned on me – had I not been promoted to sergeant a few weeks earlier, I too could have been there when the bomb fell.

Although I survived two near misses that day, I actually did not get off scot free. On my way back to HQ, an elderly lady, spying my RAF uniform, came bustling up to me brandishing her walking stick. "Look what they have done to our beautiful town!" she screamed. "Why weren't you up there stopping them?" But before I could explain that I was only on the ground staff, she started walloping me about my head and shoulders, this unknowingly inflicting more damage to my person than Jerry had been unsuccessfully attempting over the past four years. Oh yes! I remember Bournemouth on that sunny Sunday in May 1943 all too well!

Francis Lawford – Bournemouth Echo, May 25th 1993.

A Canadian pilot of 3 PRC remembers that "The Gardens were full of relaxing Canadian airmen, strolling about or laying on the grass and basking in the sun. I had already made my way up to our hotel and was shining my buttons. Suddenly there was a low pitched hum in the East and this began going around to the North and then West. Twenty-two Focke-Wulf Fw 190s had crossed the coast, came around behind us and made a perfect line of stern attack on the city centre, particularly the Gardens. They were so low; as they passed my window on the third floor I could look down and see the pilot's eyes in each plane. Two 500 HEs were dropped by each of the twenty two marauders and as they were pointed out to sea when they attacked it was all over within 60 seconds! A piece of shrapnel hit me on the top of the head, small but powerful. Then I passed out for a few seconds, or minutes, and when I came to there was blood streaming all down my face." He also recalls that "As the twenty two FW 190s swept low over the gardens, they raked the airmen there with machine gun fire for the total period."

Another Canadian, a bomb aimer, states "On 23rd May 1943 I had a lateish lunch at the Bowling Green (The Winter Gardens) and was strolling across the park on a beautiful Sunday afternoon. I don't recall any warning sirens but I do remember looking up at the roar of engines to see my first enemy aircraft – Focke-Wulf 190s. I was very exposed so ran across the park to the built-up area where I took shelter in the entrance to a shop. On my way I saw an airman (Australian, I believe, since he had a darker uniform) hit and spun around with a leg missing. I spent the next few minutes (seemed like hours) cursing myself for having picked such a poor shelter since I was surrounded on three sides by plate glass. Back to Bath Hill Court to confirm my survival and then I volunteered to help at the Hotel which had been hit."

Taken from *Bournemouth and the Second World War* by M.A. Edgington

....

My Auntie Louise lived at 89 Richmond Wood Road, between Charminster and Queen's Park, with my Uncle George and their daughter Connie. The house was bombed during the Sunday May 23rd bombing of the 'Bournemouth Blitz'. When the gang cleared up the site they found the fin from the bomb, which had the number 89 painted on it. My Aunt always remarked that it had her number on it!

Jim Fail. June 2012.

....

May 1943, my parents, returning from burying my grandfather in Caversham, Reading, got off the train at Central Station in Bournemouth, and proceeded down Holdenhurst Road towards the Lansdowne, where they were going to call in at the hotel Metropole for a cup of tea, before going home to 8 Durley Road, West Cliff. They had fasted from midnight. On approaching the hotel, they were met by Police Constable Brown, who knew them both as he had been at their wedding, being a friend of the family. He told them to go straight home and not go into the hotel, as he was sure that he heard a jerry plane but no siren had gone yet. He advised them to walk up the back way and not get a bus. This they did, and when they arrived home, they found my grandfather from my mother's side standing in the garden with a hoe in hand, and told him that a raid had started, so they all dived for cover to the cellars.

When the all clear siren sounded, they came up from the cellars to find the row of trees in the garden, where my grandfather had been standing, with their tops machine gunned off and a piece of shrapnel on the ground.
But more important in their minds was what had happened in the Lansdowne, and could they help in any way. My father, who was on compassionate leave from the RAF, went with my grandfather to see if they could help, and saw the full devastation of the whole event.

A week later, the services were still trying to find people trapped and came across one man who had kept himself alive by drinking from the broken spirits in the cellar where he had landed.

Not all the bodies were able to be bought out as they were too badly blown to dust, these the authority decided should remain in the cellar and were bricked up when the rebuilding was done during the war.

B. ATKIN-SPIVEY (Miss)

The following recollection is by Michael Hodges, who was in Bobby's at the time of the raid.

I was born in Plymouth (14.8.37) and lived there during the war. We were heavily bombed, the city had the highest proportion of civilian casualties of anywhere in the U.K. so I was familiar with German aircraft, noise and appearance. I had a grandmother who lived at Surrey Road, in Bournemouth and I visited her for a holiday. On the day in question, my parents and I were lunching at Bobby's the big shop in the square. We sat at glass topped tables in front of the window on the second floor (I think) at the front of the building overlooking the square.

I heard the sound of a Focke Wulf, single engined clipped wing German Fighter Bomber. I said to my Dad, "Jerries". He said, "There's been no siren." Then I saw the aircraft coming in low, about the height of the Pier. They had to climb to reach bombing height. The sirens went off as I saw into the cockpit of one of the aircraft as it banked and climbed. I saw the bomb hung underneath leave the aircraft. This was followed by an explosion and a cloud of dust, smoke and rubble in the air. I did not see the building it hit, as others were in my line of sight. Later I discovered it was the Metropole Hotel, which was used by the Canadian Air Force.

My mother tried to push me under the table (we did this at home in Plymouth when machine gunned and no time to reach the shelter in the back yard). I pointed out that it was glass topped. My father took us out of the restaurant and downstairs just before the windows blew in.

We stood outside Bobbys in the narrow alley between it and the next building to its north side. More bombs, machine guns and fire engine bells, then the all clear sounded and we went back to Surrey Road.

Because Plymouth had been blitzed I was used to the sounds. My school had a barrage balloon on the cricket pitch. One Saturday it was shot down, I was pushed out the way of the falling cable. The balloon was replaced by a 40mm Bofors A/A gun. The older boys in the Army Cadets were used to carry clips of ammunition to the gun for the soldiers in the gun crew. We younger boys were keen to do the same, but were never old enough.

My mother had once picked up an incendiary bomb which had come through the front room window; she used the fire tongs to put it in the garden to burn out. At the height of the blitz we lived in the shelter, no gas or electricity. Mother tried to cook on an open coal fire, I recall sitting in the shelter, counting the bombs either in sticks of six (250Kg), or three (500Kg), hoping they would go either side. Our windows were covered in tape to reduce the effects of blast and all external doors and windows had to be covered in blackout curtains.

On occasions going to school I would see fire and rescue crews at work, roads blocked by rubble, ruined buildings, people being dug out. So the holiday in Bournemouth did not seem to be a big deal.

Michael Hodges. 24th June 2010.

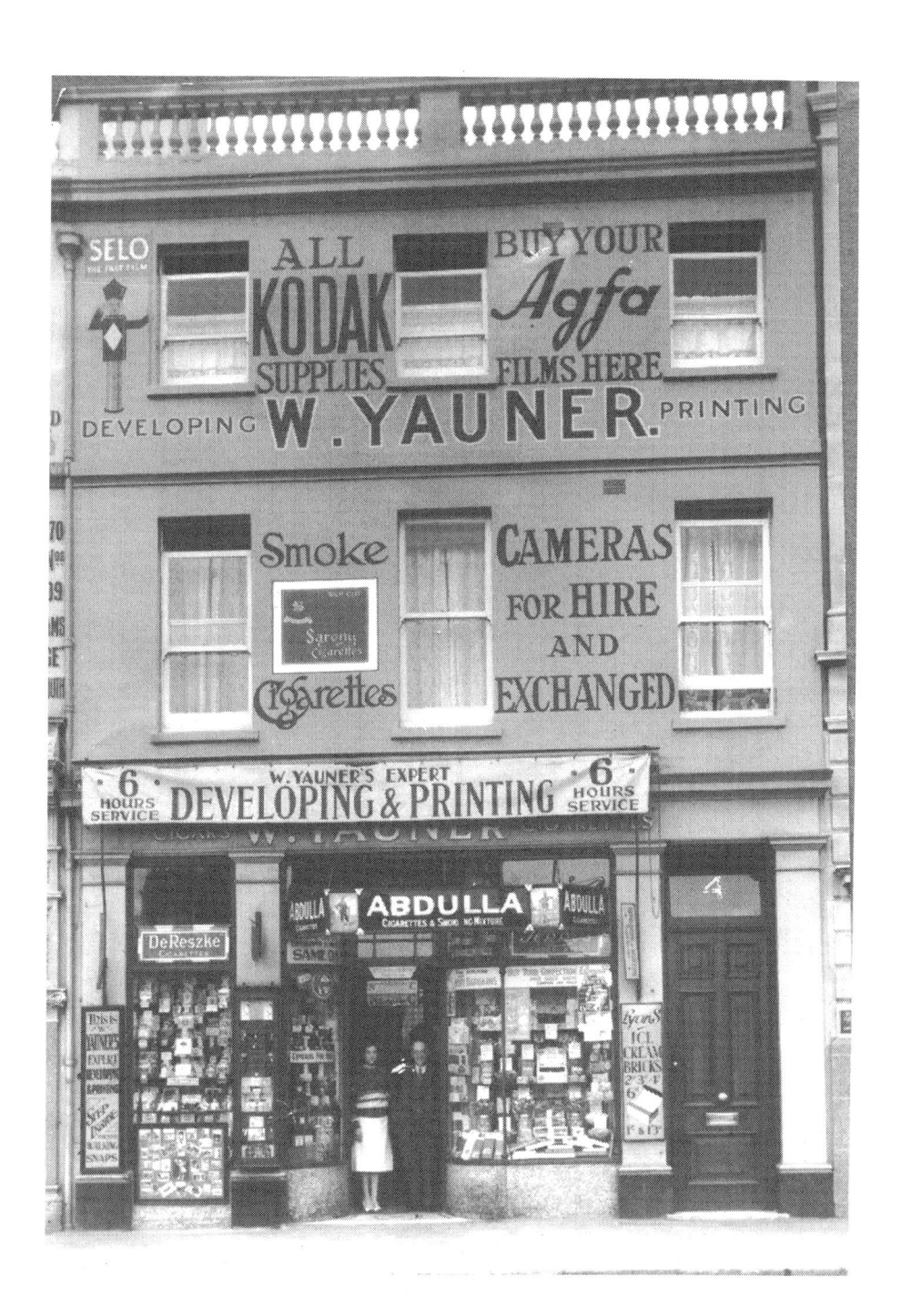

Yauners Tobacconists, Lansdowne Crescent

Mrs. Polakoff and her brother Alex Yauner outside Lansdowne Crescent (Rhona Taylor's mother and uncle)

4 LANSDOWNE CRESCENT

4 Lansdowne Crescent is one of a small group of shops that was in very close vicinity to the Metropole Hotel. At the time of the raid, it was owned by the Yauner family. They had lived there since the turn of the century where they ran a tobacconist shop. At the time of writing this study, it is currently the Post Office.

The following quotation comes from Rhona Taylor and describes her memories of that time.

> *I lived at 4 Lansdowne Crescent – in fact most of my family lived at 4 Lansdowne Crescent. Over the shop – Yauner's the Tobacconist. It was painted a horrible yellow colour. Why the colour? Because when anyone asked my grandfather why he chose such a horrible colour, he replied, "You noticed the shop." I digress.*
>
> *My father joined the Royal Navy in 1940 so my mother, my sister and I, aged four, moved in with my grandparents, aunt and uncle and two cousins. We lived on the ground floor with a kitchen and scullery. Today you would call the kitchen 'the family room'. The scullery was really the kitchen and had an enormous larder. Our bedroom was on the first floor. I shared with my mother and sister had a very small room of her own. My grandparents slept on the first floor and my aunt and uncle had the top floor. Luxury – two bedrooms, a living room, kitchen and bathroom. At*

the back of the building was a very large garden in which we, of course, grew all our own fruit and vegetables. I still remember the apple tree, gooseberry bushes along the wall and even raspberries.

My sister, Doris and I went to school on the number 27 trolley bus with instructions from mother to the conductor to put us off at Stokewood Road stop and see us across the road. In those days mothers didn't have cars to take us – no petrol of course and I don't suppose many women drove. It was all so safe with never a thought of anything nasty happening to us. When I was six we changed schools to go to St. Paul's, which is now part of the huge St. Paul's roundabout. It was much nearer home.

There were many Canadian and American serviceman billeted in Bournemouth and the Metropole Hotel, on the corner of Holdenhurst and Christchurch Roads, was used to house them as were most hotels. Bournemouth seemed very peaceful during the early part of the war with one or two bombs but nothing very serious until Sunday 23rd May 1943.

It was the day before my mother's birthday and we were going to have a family lunch to celebrate. Doris and I were playing in the garden when the siren went. Mother called us in and being obedient children we went in. It was a good job we did. We never had the lunch!!

The German planes flew very low over the town, dropping their bombs and shooting people in the street. My fourteen year old cousin, Michael, rushed out to see what was happening and was literally blown back in by the blast, six bombs had fallen around us. The Metropole which was full of Canadian airmen and lunch time visitors to the bar, which was still open, had a direct hit. Sherry and Haycock, wood suppliers, in Oxford Road was on fire, The Kingsway Hotel in Lansdowne Road was bombed. Beales, the Central Hotel and Richmond Hill Congregational Church were also flattened. Where my sister and I had played five minutes earlier, the rubble was two feet deep. Most of our windows were shattered. Mercifully none of our family was hurt.

Rhona Taylor (left) with her mother and sister Doris photographed by the Bournemouth Echo after the raid

My father had somehow heard about the raid but as he was on a destroyer on Russian Convoys somewhere in the North Atlantic, it took a while for him to know that we, at least, were still alive.

I still remember that day so clearly although I was only seven. The Red Cross set up their headquarters for making tea at the front of the house, outside the shop. They used our kettle. We never found the lid. Funny things one remembers.

There were so many killed that day and I won't go into any more details as it has been told many times, except to say that thank goodness in those days you did what your mother told you because if we hadn't, I certainly wouldn't be writing this today.

Rhona's sister Doris added the following: -

The only things I can remember, are dead people lying in the road and it was very difficult to open the front door because of the rubble. The garden was deep in debris and all our spare blankets disappeared as well as the spare kettle. The shock was tremendous and poor Dad heard about it at sea and did not know if we were safe or not. The trauma went deep. Years later when HMS Belfast fired a welcome salvo, I burst out crying.

MEMORIES FROM MADEIRA COURT

Madeira Court were Police houses in Madeira Road, at the rear of Lansdowne Crescent.

As I remember Sunday 23rd May 1943, was a pleasant sunny day. I was 10 years old and I lived with my parents and sister in a police house attached to the Police Station in Madeira Road, Bournemouth.

Angela, my cousin, who lived next door and myself were busy playing with our dolls on the back door-step of my home. In my dolls pram was the family cat fast asleep. All was well, the air raid siren had sounded but no-one seemed concerned. Then our peace was shattered. Planes were overhead, very low. I remember seeing the pilot as it passed the house. Seconds later a bomb exploded over the wall just a matter of feet from where we were playing. I do not remember any noise at the time, but there was destruction everywhere. In panic I rushed indoors to the kitchen shutting the door. My cousin Angela, tried to follow me but I would not let her in. She eventually found her way home through all the rubble and it was a miracle how we both were not killed.

I found my mother quite badly cut about the face due to flying glass from the kitchen window. After a while my father appeared. He was in the police garage and had been knocked unconscious for a short while, he found mum and I in the cupboard under the stairs. He attended to my mother's cut face.

Sometime later my sister Ruby arrived home. She worked in the Metropole Hotel which had a direct hit. She was thrown into the basement and has no idea how she escaped or survived. She was shocked as we all were and I will never forget her hair which stood on end, covered in white plaster and dust.

When we eventually emerged into the garden the damage around us was terrible. I remember mum was quite concerned, she had washing on the line and when she picked it up from the ground, every garment had a bullet hole through it. This was quite serious to lose so many clothes as they were not able to be replaced, rationing did not allow for this.

Angela, I am glad to say managed to find her way home and all of that family were shaken but well. We often speak of the ordeal of that day when we meet now. After all the terror and the confusion at the end of the day, we were still a complete family and we all recovered from the ordeal for which we were all truly thankful.

Statement by: SHEILA M.JAMES (née Hudd)

Thanks for telegram &
Pat's letter.   26/5/43.

My dear Den,
   Please excuse these few hurried lines. I hadn't forgotten your birthday on Monday, but honestly after Sun I hadn't time to write, we have been bombed out at home, and are unable to live in our house, but I think we are fixed up now. We have been up with Dais the Trek also had a direct hit whilst I was there, but luckily we all escaped without any serious injuries. Will write again when we are more settled. Love Ruby

Letter from Ruby Hudd (later Holloway)
to her future husband Dennis
3 days after the raid

Sheila's sister Ruby recalled the following: -

After leaving school in the summer of 1939 I started work in the Reception Office of the Metropole Hotel, about the second week of September. Not on the payroll the first week or so but just to gain a bit of experience of the working world. We left school at fourteen in those days (most of us) and were not given any information of life after school.

After a few weeks I was given the chance to stay and was thrilled as I loved my time there. At that time it was totally a hotel, quite a large and imposing building.

If I remember correctly, an insurance company from London moved in the early part of the war and had offices in a small part of the hotel, but the Air Force arrived and I guess the insurance company had to leave. I remember staying on in that office because the bars on the Holdenhurst Road side of the building were still open.

On the day of the 23rd I can not remember there had been an air raid warning. I had gone down to the cellar for a bottle of liquor wanted in one of the bars. I don't think there was anyone else in the cellar being Sunday, but I am not certain. I did not see anyone and I do not remember hearing any unusual noise. Suddenly the lights went out and I was thrown to the ground.

I have been led to believe that I was so close to the explosion that the blast went over my head.

Fortunately I knew my way in most parts of the hotel and eventually found my way out into Holdenhurst Road, not having seen anyone one on the way. It was very dark. I only saw one man in Holdenhurst Road, he was standing against the wall of the building opposite and appeared stunned. Neither of us spoke.

I made my way home to Madeira Court passing Mr. Yauner's shop. I met a policeman about there, whom I must have known, my father being a policeman. I remember asking him if my family were o.k. He did not answer me. I realised after that he probably didn't recognise me as my hair was white with dust and plaster. This took a long time to remove and it was some time before I could wash my hair clean again. I also had blood on my clothes but it must have been minor cuts for luckily I was not injured.

On reaching Madeira Court, my way home was blocked by a pile of rubble caused by a bomb that had landed over the wall behind the shops in Lansdowne Road (the Post Office, butchers hairdressers etc). I climbed over this and found my mother and sister sheltering in the cupboard under the stairs.

In the early days of the war, if the air raid sirens sounded in the evening or the night, the wives and children (I was one of them) of the seven police houses would cross the police yard and go under the Law Court building in Stafford Road. The young ones had collapsible beds and we would stay there until the all clear sounded.

We had to move out of that house until it was fit to live in again and had a few rooms at 28 Dean Park Road, where the police had offices at the time.

Mr and Mrs Wilson were living in Queens Park and I went there for a while in the mornings after the bombing. Mr Wilson then found me a job in the reception office of the Grand Hotel in Fir Vale Road. I stayed there until that was also requisitioned for Polish and Free French Army and Navy Officers, and officers from other occupied countries. By then the bars of the Metropole had re- opened and I had a small office where I did the office work, letters wages etc., until I was called up for war work.

Ruby Holloway (née Hudd) May 2011

Angela, who was aged 5 years at the time, remembers the following: -

It was Sunday may 23rd, 1943, near lunchtime, when my cousin Sheila, who lived next door to us (my parents and myself), in the police houses in Madeira Court, Madeira Road, Bournemouth, and myself were playing with our dolls and Sheila's cat in a pram in the back yard.

My father was P.C.397 Albert Victor Newton King (nicknamed Joe) and Sheila's father, P.C. William Hudd were both policemen. He, together with my mother, was brother and sister - William Hudd and Ellen Mary Hudd – William nicknamed "Will" and Ellen Mary "Nan". The Hudd family from Winchester, Hants consisted of 11 police officers, including my father. The largest police family in the British Isles.

On this particular sunny Sunday lunchtime, we were both playing very happily when suddenly the air raid siren sounded. We knew exactly what that meant, that German war planes were approaching. Sheila ran indoors and I ran to her back door continually knocking but could not make anyone hear. I turned to approach Sheila's small, wooden yard gate to go through my own yard gate and run into my own home, only to be stopped in my tracks by the sight of a very low flying German plane coming towards me. I saw the pilot and the bomb clearly leave the plane, which landed the other side of the long brick wall which divided police accommodation from the backs of the Lansdowne road shops and the flats above.

I was blasted towards the brick wall and was subsequently buried underneath it. When I gradually realised what had happened, I pushed the bricks away from myself to get out into daylight eventually. I stood up, looked around and saw a thick dusty atmosphere all around and looked up at the flats in Lansdowne Road, which I could just about make-out through the dusty haze and it looked first like someone had opened up a large wall of a very big house and you could see a light in all of the different rooms, beds, bedding, wardrobes, tables, chairs, curtaining, ceilings, clothing, kitchen cooker etc. Etc. all perched at very precarious angles, over the edges of the floors, just hanging and all over the place in the rooms of each property, wide open for all to see, and a very musty smell hung heavily around the whole area. I recall tripping over my aunties clothes line (rope) and made my way round to the front of my home and on passing tried to locate Charlie, my cousin's tortoise, to make sure he was alright, but I couldn't find him in his usual place.

I crawled and scrambled over debris around to my own front door, to be met by my father's open arms; he said thank god you are safe and gave me a long cuddle. I later learned that my mother was evidently walking towards our back door, through the kitchen, to call me in when the blast of the bomb threw her back onto the kitchen floor and knocked her out.

We eventually all joined together in Sheila's parents lounge and Sheila and I were put in the indoor 'cage-like' shelter to rest until the police doctor came, Doctor Coleman who resided at St. Peters Hill, Winton, Bournemouth, Dorset.

We removed pieces of glass and shrapnel from each other's hair and clothing and I recall my mother asking Sheila if she would kindly read a Rupert book to keep me awake as I was on no account to go to sleep, and bless her, she read and read and read until Doctor Coleman eventually arrived.

I recall my cousin Ruby, Sheila's elder sister, entering auntie's kitchen and we were all so happy to see her, although, as we all were, covered in white dust. Ruby looked just like a ghost, her hair was all stood on end and her lovely blue jacket had a very dark stain down the front. Ruby was a receptionist at the Metropole Hotel, at the Lansdowne, which had a direct hit and many American soldiers died. How Ruby survived, as she was in the cellar at the time the bomb dropped directly on to the Metropole Hotel, we'll never know as she cannot recall fully how she got out of the Metropole to walk home. She passed two people both of whom did not speak.

One thing that was referred to quite frequently after the bombing was the fact that Sheila had an English doll and I had a German doll. They were left side- by-side on auntie's doorstep. After the bomb dropped, Sheila's doll was blown to pieces and mine was completely unscathed. I have only just learnt that all my aunt's washing on her clothes line was peppered with bullet holes and I know realise what a truly narrow escape I had.

Later my father took me to the massive hole where the bomb had landed. My mother took me down to see Beales. Sights of which will remain with me for the rest of my days. Especially when one passes an old building which is being pulled down for development. When one passes that same horrid musty smell, living memories come flooding back.
It was all quite an experience and to this day I am not able to watch a war film.

Statement by: Angela Bradford (née King)

"DAD"
VICTOR
DOUGLAS
HERRIDGE
KILLED BY
ENEMY ACTION
"MUM"
LILIAN
FLORENCE
HERRIDGE
DIED

CIVILIAN DEAD

The following civilians are recorded as having died due to enemy action in Bournemouth on 23rd May 1943

ADLEM Reginald George   Aged 43
Died at Shamrock and Rambler garage.
Motor Engineer.
Of 7 Orcheston Road.
Husband of Hilda Adlem.
Buried 27th May. Wimborne Road Cemetery. G4/96s

BAKER Lilian Maud   Aged 57
Died at Metropole Hotel.
Of 24 Purbeck Road.
Wife of Cyril John Baker (Dental Mechanic).
Daughter of Sidney Horatio Herbert.
Buried Wimborne Road Cemetery. J4/97s

BIRCHAM Maud Violet   Aged 47
Died at Central Hotel.
W.V.S.
Wife of Raymond Frank Bircham.
Daughter of Mr and Mrs J.H. Murgatroyd of Ipswich.

BIRCHAM Raymond Frank   Aged 45
Died at Central Hotel.
Royal Observer Corps, N.P. Bank Accountant.
Of "Covehithe" Newmarket Road, Bury St, Edmunds, Suffolk.
Son of Mr and Mrs. H.W. Bircham of Brundall, Norfolk.

BLOUNT Eliza Minnie   Aged 68
Died at 20, Bethia Road.
Servant.
Buried 28th May. North Cemetery. G4/65

BLOWER Walter Ernest   Aged 56
Died at Metropole Hotel.
Civil Servant.
Of 211 Phipps Bridge Road, Merton, London.
Husband of Mollie Mason Blower.
Buried 28th May. London Road, Mitcham

BOWIE Catherine   Aged 74
Died at Royal Victoria Hospital, Boscombe.
Of 12 Lansdowne Road.
Widow of Lewis John Bowie.
Daughter of James and Elizabeth Durran.

BROWN William Henry   Aged 53
Died at Howard Road.
Air Raid Warden.
Retired commercial traveller.
Husband of Grace Brown, of 31 Cecil Ave.

BROWNE Agnes Louise   Aged 30
Died at Central Hotel (basement).
Of 6 Trafalgar Road.
Wife of L.A.C Cyril Browne.
Buried 29th May. Wimborne Road Cemetery. A4/100s

BROWNE Thomas John M.B.   Aged 91
Died at Royal Victoria Hospital, Boscombe.
Retired Doctor Of Killymaddy, C. Tyrone.
Husband of Jane Donaldson Browne.
Son of late William and Anne Browne.

BUDDEN Frances   Aged 76
Died at 60 Richmond Wood Road.
Of 287 Seely Road.
Widow of George Henry Budden (Storekeeper).
Buried 28th May. Langton Matravers

CALLAN Albert Edward   Aged 41
Injured at Central Hotel. Died, Royal Victoria Hospital, Boscombe.
Jam Manufacturer.
Husband of Mrs.Dorothy Irene Callan.
Son of Mrs Callan of King Edwards Road, Malvern Wells.

CALLAN Dorothy Irene   Aged 32
Died at Central Hotel.
Of Ledbury Preserves, Ledbury, Hereford.
Wife of Edward Callan (Jam Manufacturer).
Daughter of Mr. Albert E. & Mrs. L.M.Jones of Little Marcle.
Buried 31st May. Malvern Wells.

CANDY Dorothy Kent   Aged 47
Died at Cairns House.
Hotel Assistant.
Widow of Major R.G.L.Candy, R.F.C.
Daughter of Arthur and Mary Littlepair of Newcastle-on-Tyne.
Buried 2nd June. North Cemetery. N4/65

CHAPMAN Donald John Salter Aged 54
Died at Royal Victoria Hospital, Boscombe.
Husband of V.M.Chapman of 6, Jervis Road.

CLARK Barbara Christine Aged 17
Died at Royal Victoria Hospital, Boscombe.
Of Kingsway Hotel, 12 Lansdowne Road.
Daughter of the late Stanley Clark.
Step daughter of J. Kater.
Buried 31st May. East Cemetery. L4/55

CLYNE Grace Condon M.A. Aged 42
Died at Howard Road.
A.R.P. Telephonist.
Widow of Christopher Clyne.
Daughter of William H and Beatrice Addison
of 163 Richmond Park Road.

COLE Clement John Aged 50
Injured at 56 Drummond Road.
Died at Royal Victoria Hospital, Boscombe.
Brewers Helper.
Husband of Mrs. A. J. Cole.
Buried 31st May. East Cemetery. O4/55

COLLEN Eleanor Ida Sinclair Aged 61
Died at 20, Bethia Road.
Widow of William Collen (County Surveyor).
Daughter of Thomas John and Sara Henderson Brown.
Buried 29th May. East Cemetery. J4/172

CRUTE Jean   Aged 22
Died at Central Hotel.
Of 4a Knowles Hill Rd, Newton Abbott.
Wife of Lieutenant Leonard Robert Edmonds Crute R.E.
Daughter of Reginald John and Mable Badcock.

DAWES Annie   Aged 65
Died at Hotel Metropole.
Domestic Help. (Kingsway Hotel)
Of 12 Lansdowne Road.
Buried 29th May. North Cem. J4/65

DELLER Phyllis Emily   Aged 28
Died at Hotel Metropole.
Of The Corner House, Lansdowne.
Wife of Sapper Arthur Henry Deller R.E.
Daughter of Mrs. E Rice.
Buried 29th May. Wimborne Road Cem. E4/60s

DIMASCIO Pamela Clara   Aged 43
Died at rear of 248 Holdenhurst Road.
Of 250 Holdenhurst Road.
Wife of Jack Dimascio (Cycle Maker).
Buried 31st May. Wimborne Road. S6/52s

DIMASCIO Sylvia   Aged 9
Died at Methuen Road.
Of 250 Holdenhurst Road.
Daughter of Jack and Pamela Dimascio.
Buried 31st May. Wimborne Road. S6/52s

DOLTON Charles Stanley   Aged 54
Died at Hotel Metropole.
Grocer's Assistant.
Of 62 Darracott Road.
Son of the late George Hames Dolton.
Buried 27th May. North Cemetery. B4/65

DYSON Beryl   Aged 23
Died at Central Hotel.
Of 45 School Road, Moseley, Birmingham.
Daughter of Mr. and Mrs. Joseph William Dyson.
Buried 31st May. Yardley Wood, Birmingham.

EGGETT Henry George   Aged 73
Died at 54 Drummond Road.
Husband of Christiana Eggett.
Buried 28th May. East Cemetery. U5/145

EVISON Harriett Maria   Aged 70
Died at Kingsway Hotel.
Of 12 Lansdowne Road.
Widow of Simon Evison (Kitchen Porter).
Buried 29th May. North Cemetery. B3/93

FLYNN Bernard   Aged 41
Died at Central Hotel.
Home Guard, Telephone Engineer.
Husband of Catherine Flynn.
Son of Mrs. M.A.Flynn and the late J. Flynn.

FLYNN Catherine Barbara   Aged 40 (34?)
Died at Central Hotel.
Of 12 Crescent Road.
Wife of Bernard Flynn.
Buried 1st June. Guildford.

FORSYTH George Foley   Aged 62
Died at Central Hotel.
Civil Servant.
Of 12 St. Stephen's Mount, Richmond Hill.
Husband of Mable Florence Forsyth.
Son of the late Rev.T.J.Forsyth.
Buried 28th May. Wimborne Road Cemetery. D4/50s

HARTIN Julia   Aged 47
Died at 38 Carlton Road.
Daughter of the late Mr. and Mrs. N.W.Hartin.
(lost her life in saving evacuated children)

HARVEY Harold Albert Michael   Aged 44
Died at Central Hotel.
Air Raid Warden.
Australian Agent for British, Australian and N.Z. newspaper.
Of 46 Kings Road, New Haw, Addlestone, Surrey.
Husband of Foris Annie Harvey.

HASLER Frederick Edward   Aged 49
Injured at Central Hotel.
Died at Royal Victoria Hospital Boscombe.
Swiss Citizen of 48 Barton Road, Branksome.
Son of the late Margaret Hasler.

HAWKE Florence Eva   Aged 41
Died at 54 Drummond Road.
Wife of Leslie Hawke (Engineer).
Buried 27th May. East Cemetery. E4/55

HAWKE Pamela   Aged 10
Died at 54 Drummond Road.
Daughter of Leslie and Florence Eva Hawke. (father, Engineer)
Buried 27th May. East Cemetery. E4/55

HAWKE Wendy   Aged 8
Died at 54 Drummond Road.
Daughter of Leslie and Florence Eva Hawke. (father, Engineer)
Buried 27th May East Cemetery. E4/55

HAYWARD Michael Douglas   Aged 10
Died at 22 Bethia Road.
Son of Douglas Wilfred & Isabel Rosser Hayward. (father, Builder)
Buried 26th May. East Cemetery. R4/17

HERRIDGE Douglas Victor   Aged 39
Died at Beales.
Home Guard, Torpedo Fitter.
Of 36 Shirley Road.
(killed by falling rubble whilst on duty)

HOFFENBERG Harry — Aged 50
Died at The Metropole Hotel.
Jeweller's Traveller.
Of The Corner House, Lansdowne.
Son of B Hoffenberg.
Buried 27th May. New Synagogue, Wimston?

HOOPER Cynthia Betty — Aged 17
Died at Drop-in-Café, 41 Cleveland Road.
Of 41/43 Cleveland Road.
Daughter of Lily E.N.Hooper and the late Walter Hooper (Labourer)
Buried 28th May. East Cemetery. G4/55

HOWARD Eileen (Spinster) — Aged 52
Died at Normandie Hotel, 61 Manor Road.
Of White House, West Dean, Salisbury.
Daughter of the late George Charles Howard.
Buried 27th May, Whiteparish, Wiltshire.

JEFFREY Kathleen — Aged 37
Died at The Metropole Hotel.
Of 6 Undercliffe Road.
Wife of Lt. Harry Cecil Jeffrey R.A.F.
Buried 28th May. East Cemetery. E4/18

KATER Barbara Christine — Aged 41
Died at Royal Victoria Hospital, Boscombe.
Of 12 Lansdowne Road.
Wife of John Kater. Died 29th May.
Buried 31st May. East Cemetery. L4/55

KEEN Dorothy May   Aged 30
Died at Central Hotel.
A.R.P. Ambulance Driver.
Of 275 Devizes Road, Salisbury Wiltshire.
Wife of Sgt. G.L. Keen, Royal Army Service Corps.

KERSLAKE John James   Aged 63
Died at Central Hotel.
Labourer.
Of 52 Olga Road, Dorchester.
Husband of Elizabeth Ann Kerslake.
Son of the late John James and Lesh Kerslake
Buried 27th May. Dorchester.

LALLY Josephine   Aged 51
Died at Holdenhurst Road.
Of 43 Village Way, Pinner.
Wife of Peter Martin Lally.
Daughter of the late Mr. and Mrs. John Mirrilees.
Buried 26th May. Wimborne Road Cemetery. Q6/60s

LAWTON Agnes Elizabeth   Aged 57
Died at 2, Pavilion Road.
Wife of Ernest Aubrey Lawton (Chemist).
Daughter of James and Martha Blight.
Buried 27th May. North Cemetery. K2/46

LITMAN Florence Ethel   Aged 55
Died at Central Hotel.
Spinster, Hotel Housekeeper. Central Hotel.
Buried 29th May. North Cemetery. H4/65

McGAVIN Capt. (Retired) Nathan M.C.　　　Aged 46
(Royal Ulster Rifles)
Died at Central Hotel.
Of Studleigh Rotal, Upper Terrace Road.
Husband of Olive Henrietta Templeman McGavin.
Son of the late S. McGavin.
Buried 28th May. East Cemetery. Y4/17

McHARTIN　　Julia　　　Aged 45
Died at Royal Victoria Hospital, Boscombe. (Pronounced dead on arrival)
Spinster, Boarding House Keeper.
Of 38 Carlton Road.
Buried 28th May. East Cemetery. D4/18

McTERNAN Alfred　　　Aged 41
Died at The Metropole Hotel.
Lorry Driver.
Of 163 Old Christchurch Road.
Husband of M McTernan.
Buried 27th May. North Cemetery. D4/65

MANFIELD Annie　　　Aged 65
Died at 56 Drummond Road.
Daughter of Whitwell and Sarah Manfield.
Buried 29th May. East Cemetery. K4/55

MARSH John　　　Aged 61
Died at The Metropole Hotel.
Labourer.
Of 19 Victoria Place.
Buried 29th May. East Cemetery. J2/197

MASON Lilian Mabel   Aged 40
Died at Central Hotel.
Air Raid Warden.
Of 27 Richmond Hill Chambers.
Wife of John A. Mason, Merchant Navy.

PEREGRINE Maimie Dorothy   Aged 27
Died at Central Hotel.
Air Raid Warden.
Wife of Cpl. William John Peregrine, R.A.F. of 17 The Oval, Burn Bridge, Harrogate, Yorkshire.
Daughter of Dick and Doreen Francis of Kenton, Middlesex.

PETHYBRIDGE Harold   Aged 63
Died at Central Hotel.
Home Guard.
Of Ealing London.
Son of H.J. Pethybridge of 18 Bridge Street, Chichester.

PIPER Nellie Rose   Aged 42
Died at Central Hotel.
Wife of George J Piper (Hotel Proprietor).
Daughter of Mrs Dunham.
Buried 31st May. Burton Bradstock.

POUGHER Mabel   Aged 26
Died at 56 Drummond Road.
Wife of Ernest Pougher, Cpl. (7666566) R.A.P.C.
Buried St. Mary's Church, Beverley, Yorkshire.

ROBSHAW Robert Barrington   Aged 37(35?)
Died at Central Gardens.
Radio Distributor.
Of Oakmist Garage, Mount Ephrain, Tunbridge Wells.
Husband of Mabel Robshaw.
Son of Robert Benjamin and Minnie Robshaw
Cremated 26th May.

ROGERS Hubert Edgar   Aged 50
Died at Royal Victoria Hospital, Boscombe.
Of 14 Curzon Road, Poole.
Died 24th May 1943.

SCHOFIELD Lawrence Herbert   Aged 59
Died at Central Hotel.
Hotel Proprietor.
Of The Central Hotel.
Buried 28th May. Wimborne Road Cemetery. O7/2n

SIKES Howard Lecky C.B.E.   Aged 61
Died at Central Hotel.
Senior Regional Technical Advisor, Ministry of Home Security.
Husband of Elsie Priscilla Sikes.

SMOOTHY Lily   Aged 28
Died at Hotel Metropole.
Aircraft Fitter.
Of 9 Farrer Street, Nelson, Burnley & The Bungalow, Ely Road, Streatham, Ely.
Daughter of Joseph and Eliza Ann Smoothy.
Buried 30th May. Stretham, Isle of Ely.

SPINAK Abraham (Albert)   Aged 41
Died at Central Gardens.
Musician.
Of Meriville Hotel, Exeter Road.
Husband of Constance Spinak.
Son of Soloman and Bertha Spinak.
Buried 27th May. East Cemetery. G6/157

STOCKTON Edith Constance   Aged 38
Died at 248A, Holdenhurst Road.
Newsagent and Tobacconist.
Daughter of Edith and the late William Henry Stockton.
Buried 31st May. East Cemetery. H4/55

THOMAS Florence   Aged 29
Died at Central Hotel.
Waitress.
Of 20b Edmondsham House, Terrace Road.
Wife of Richard James Thomas.
Buried 27th May. North Cemetery. F4/65

THROWER Henry Steven   Aged 72
Died at Central Hotel.
Of 10 Surrey Road.

TODD Barbara Jean   Aged 20
Died at The Metropole Hotel.
W.T.C.
Of 5 Downs Road, Purley Surrey.
Wife of L/Cpl. Richard Fredrick Todd. R.E.

TRENT Mary Frances　　　　　　　　　　　　　　Aged 30
Died at Central Hotel.
Spinster, Shorthand Typist.
Of 39 Copse Edge Avenue, Epsom.
Daughter of Alfred and Jessie Trent.
Buried 2nd June. North Cemetery. M4/65

VAUGHAN William Henry　　　　　　　　　　Aged 51
Died outside The Metropole Hotel.
A.R.P. Rescue Service. Corporation Employee.
Husband of Elizabeth Vaughan of 142 Old Christchurch Road.

VINCENT George William　　　　　　　　　　Aged 33
Died at Metropole Hotel.
Radio Engineer.
Of Tower Hill, Willerton, Somerset.
Husband of Doris E Vincent.
Son of Mrs A. Vincent and the late A. Vincent.
Buried 29th May. Croscombe, Somerset.

WALTON George William　　　　　　　　　　Aged 50
Died at Shamrock and Rambler Garage, Holdenhurst Road.
Garage Attendant.
Husband of Ethel Walton.
Buried 28th May. Wimborne Road Cemetery. E4/72s.

WEBB Marriott Webb D.C.M.　　　　　　　　Aged 45
Died at Central Hotel.
Home Guard, Bank Clerk.
Husband of Lily Webb of 72 Halifax Drive, Westcliff on Sea, Essex.

WEBSTER Annie Christian   Aged 70
Died at 39, Cleveland Road.
Wife of Walter Clarke Webster
Buried 31st May. East Cemetery. G4/18

WELLER Edward   Aged 75
Died at Central Hotel.
Head Waiter.
Husband of Amelia Weller
Buried 29th May. East Cemetery. M3/226

WESTBROOK Beryl   Aged 21
Died at 56 Drummond Road.
Wife of Leslie Westbrook, H.M.Forces.
Buried 31st May. East Cemetery. O4/55

WHEELER Michael Geoffrey   Aged 21months
Died at Cairns House, St. Peter's Road.
Of 16 Bourne Valley Road.
Son of Maurice Henry and Valerie Wheeler.
(40th R.T.C., Head Waiter), (mother's maiden name Candy)
Buried 2nd June. North Cemetery.

WHITWELL Beatrice Lamb   Aged 44
Died at 29 Vale Road.
Wife of James Sylvester Whitwell (Jeweller).
Buried 27th May. East Cemetery. W4/55

WOOLLARD Roger George   Aged 4
Died at 38 Carlton Road.
Son of Pte. Herbert Samual Woollard R.A.P.C (7915173) and D F Woollard.
Buried 27th May. Wimborne Road Cemetery. C4/88s

WORMELL Lilian Maud   Aged 60
Died at Normandie Hotel.
Of White House, West Dean, Salisbury.
Widow of Robert Alfred Wormell.
Buried 27th May. Whiteparish, Wiltshire.

MILITARY DEAD

The following are recorded as having died due to the enemy action on May 23rd 1943.

ROYAL AIR FORCE

| Name | Service No. | Age |

AC1 William Stevens Anthony   1631292   40 yrs
Royal Air Force Volunteer Reserve.
Died at
Buried at Stapleford Cemetery, Section A, Grave 515.

LAC Charles Arthur William Bailey 1080166   31 yrs
Royal Air Force Volunteer Reserve.
Died at The Metropole Hotel.
Husband of M.G. Bailey.
Son of Arthur John and Eleanor Bailey of Winchester.
Body unrecovered.
Memorial entry on Panel 17, Runnymede Memorial.

Sgt. William Herbert Bastable   1433876   22 yrs
Royal Air Force Volunteer Reserve.
(Navigator/Bomber)
Died at
Son of Herbert Arthur and Edith Ellen Bastable of Heaton Mersey, Lancashire.
Buried Ledbury Cemetery, Section U.V, Row 11A/12A Grave 91/92.

LAC Philip Lawson Corner 1066878 40 yrs
Royal Air Force Volunteer Reserve.
Died at
Son of William Gladstone Corner and Emma White Corner, of Whitby.
Buried Whitby Cemetery. Grave 4022.

LAC Ronald Crawshaw 1026511 34 yrs
Royal Air Force Volunteer Reserve.
Died at The Metropole Hotel.
Son of Fred and Hannah Marie Crawshaw, of Hebden Bridge, Yorkshire.
Buried North Cemetery, Row G4, Grave 94.

AC2 Thomas Hayde 1651763 22 yrs
Royal Air Force Volunteer Reserve.
Died at
Buried Bury Cemetery, Section. H.P. 138, Grave 6249.

Sgt. Frederick William Hennessy 1551026 23 yrs
Royal Air Force Volunteer Reserve.
Died at
Son of James Henry and Mabel Husdon Hennessey, of Edinburgh.
His Brother James Wallace Hennessey, also died on service.
Buried Edinburgh Rosebank Cemetery, Section C, Grave 33.

LAC Jack Howlett 1657723 38 yrs
Royal Air Force Volunteer Reserve
Died at The Metropole Hotel
Son of Charles Robert and Ellen Howlett of Leytonstone, Essex.
Buried North Cemetery, Row D4, Grave 94.

LAC James Ireland   1057613   21 yrs
Royal Air Force Volunteer Reserve.
Died at
Son of David and Joan Ireland of Lochee, Dundee.
Buried at Dundee (Balgay) Cemetery, Plot A, Grave 196.

AC2 Andrew Joseph Lohoar   1862704   45 yrs
Royal Air Force Volunteer Reserve.
Died at The Metropole Hotel.
Husband of E.P Lohoar of Grays, Essex.
Buried North Cemetery, Row U3, Grave 95.

LAC Vincent Monaghan   1056266   23 yrs
Royal Air Force Volunteer Reserve.
Died at
Son of Bernard and Margaret Monaghan, of Wigan.
Buried Wigan Cemetery, Section J.R.C., Grave 1045.

AC1 James Joseph Morrissey   1486216   39 yrs
Royal Air Force Volunteer Reserve.
Died at The Metropole Hotel.
Son of Thomas and Mary Morrissey of Tramore, Co.Waterford, Irish Republic. Husband of Josephine M. Morrissey of Tramore.
Buried North Cemetery, Row K4, Grave 99.

Wilfred John Peregrine   1165661   32 yrs(31)
Royal Air Force Volunteer Reserve.
Died at
Husband of M.D. Peregrine. 17 The Oval, Burbridge, Harrowgate.
Son of William and Anne Elizabeth Peregrine of Roundhay, Leeds.
Buried Roundhay (St. Johns) Church, Ref. B., Grave 35. 31st May 1943.

LAC Charles Dennis Pulsford   1462593   21 yrs
Royal Air Force Volunteer Reserve.
Died at
Son of Charles George William and Violet Louisa Pulsford of Stamford-Le-Hope.
Buried Thurruck Cemetery, Section A, Grave 254.

LAC Ralph Taylor   1415453   20 yrs
Royal Air Force Volunteer Reserve
Died at
Son of Ernest Augustus and Flossie Taylor of Aberdare.
Buried at Aberdare Cemetery, Grave W/32/27.

Unidentified Airman   -   -
Body recovered from The Metropole Hotel.
Buried North Cemetery on 29th May. Plot T3/99.

ROYAL AUSTRALIAN AIR FORCE

Name	Service No.	Age

Sgt. Colin Bernard Crabbe A420453 23 yrs
Flight Sergeant.
Died at The Central Hotel.
Son of George Bernard and Myrtle Evelyn Crabbe, of Suva Fiji.
Buried North Cemetery, Row H4, Grave 94.

Sgt. Ronald Franklin Fenton A412938 20 yrs
Flight Sergeant.
Died at The Central Hotel.
Son of Claude and Martha Fenton, of Glenn Innes, New South Wales, Australia.
Buried North Cemetery, Row F4, Grave 94.

Sgt. Neal Morton Gray A420618 19 yrs
Died at The Central Hotel
Son of Charles Leslie and Annie Catherine Gray, of Mascot, New South Wales, Australia
Buried North Cemetery, Row G4, Grave 94.

Sgt. Allan John Kerrigan A420681 24 yrs
Flight Sergeant.
Died at The Central Hotel.
Son of Norman and Sarah May Kerrigan, of Merrylands, New South Wales, Australia.
Buried North Cemetery, Row J4, Grave 94.

Sgt. John Francis McMahon   A409848   28 yrs
Flight Sergeant.
Died at The Central Hotel.
Son of John Joseph and Margaret Mattie McMahon. Husband of Muriel Edith McMahon of Oakleigh, Victoria Australia.
Buried North Cemetery, Row K4, Grave 94.

Sgt. George Arthur Mills   A33250   23 yrs
Died at The Central Hotel.
Son of George Francis and Eve Mills of Dubbo, New South Wales, Australia.
Husband of Philomena Mavis Mills of Dubbo.
Buried North Cemetery, Row E4, Grave 94.

Sgt. Vivian Lewis Pope   A416993   19 yrs
Flight Sergeant.
Died at The Central Hotel.
Son of Albert Henry and Mary Annie Pope of Waikerie, South Australia.
Buried North Cemetery, Row U3, Grave 99.

Military cortèges going to Bournemouth Cemetery

Military funerals at Bournemouth Cemetery

Military Burials at Bournemouth Cemetery

Military Burials at Bournemouth Cemetery

The Military graveyard at Bournemouth Cemetery

ROYAL CANADIAN AIR FORCE

Name	Service No.	Age

Sgt. William Geoffrey Abbott   R100271   21 yrs
(Flight Sgt 408 Sqn. Air Gunner.)
Died at The Metropole Hotel.
Son of William Geoffrey and Emily Atkinson Abbott, of Winnipeg, Manitoba, Canada.
Buried North Cemetery, Row C4, Grave 94.

Sgt. George Assaf   R120876   26 yrs
(Flight Sgt 408 Sqn. Wireless Air Gunner)
Died at The Metropole Hotel.
From McCord, Saskatchewan, Canada.   D.o.b. 27.12.16.
Buried North Cemetery, Row A4, Grave 99.

Sgt. David Rainnie Chalmers   R71447   38 yrs
Died at The Metropole Hotel.
Son of Samuel Chalmers and of Rose. E Chalmers (nee Claydon). Husband of Barbara V. Chalmers of Osoyoos, British Columbia, Canada.
Buried North Cemetery, Row D4, Grave 99.

Sgt. Robert Richard Courtney   R52252   39 yrs
(Air Gunner)
Died at The Metropole Hotel
Son of Arthur W. Courtney and Ethel Louisa Courtney of Dagenham, Essex.
Buried Bournemouth North Cem. Row F4 Grave 99.

LAC Earle Oscar Milton Gilbert R189181 26 yrs
Died at The Metropole Hotel.
Husband of Victoria Denise Gilbert of Vancouver, British Columbia, Canada. From Coalhurst, Alberta
Buried East Cemetery, Row J4, Grave 99.

Sgt. Alexander Colin Matheson R112402 20 yrs
(Air Gunner)
Died at The Metropole Hotel.
Son of Angus and Mary Elizabeth Matheson, of Glen William, Prince Edward Island, Canada.
Buried North Cemetery, Row B4, Grave 99.

Sgt. Francis John Matier R164447 32 yrs
(Air Gunner)
Died at The Metropole Hotel.
Son of John Slater Matier and Jenet Matier (nee McLarty) of Steveston, British Columbia, Canada.
Buried North Cemetery, Row C4, Grave 99.

Sgt. Raymond Francis Pelrine R88040 20 yrs
Died at The Metropole Hotel.
Son Charles M. Pelrine and Clara Pelrine of Havre Boucher Antigonish Co., Nova Scotia, Canada.
Buried North Cemetery, Row H4, Grave 99.

Sgt. Julian Louis Soos R156843 20 yrs
(Flt. Sgt. 408 Sqn. Wireless Air Gunner)
Died at The Metropole Hotel.
From Crowland, Ontario.
Buried North Cemetery, Row A4, Grave 95.

Sgt. William Godfrey Wood   R61915   29 yrs
Died at The Metropole Hotel.
Son of James Golder Wood and Alice Ashby Wood of Brancepeth, Saskatchewan, Canada.
Buried North Cemetery, Row B4, Grave 99.

Sgt. Ross Clifton Woods   R93015   25 yrs
(Clerk)
Died at The Metropole Hotel.
Son of Edward Clifton Woods and Colinnette Woods of Toronto, Ontario, Canada.
Buried at North Cemetery, Row E4, Grave 99.

OTHER SERVICE PERSONNEL

Name	Service No.	Age

Staff Sgt. Norman Ellis Baker   10596343   N/ Known
108 Coy. R.E.M.E. Bovington.   Height 6ft.2in.
Body forwarded to next of kin (father).
Died at:
Body forwarded to next of kin (father) Ashton-Under-Lyne, Lancs.
Correspondence dated Sept. 1944 ref. to body being disinterred, cremated and the ashes to be sent to South Africa.
Buried Ndola (Kansenshi) Cemetery. Zambia.
Grave Ref, Plot 1, Row B, Grave 20.

Lance Corp. Walter Carson   5190321   29 yrs
Corps of Military Police.
Died at The Central Hotel.
Son of Walter and Ada Carson, of Tranmere, Birkenhead.
Buried Birkenhead (Flaybrick Hill) Cemetery.
Grave Ref, Section 9 C of E, 322A.

Leonard Robert Edmund Crute   190957   25 yrs
Lieut. 26 Searchlight Regt., Royal Artillery.
Died at The Central Hotel.
(body recovered 24th May)
Of 4a Knowles Hill Road, Newton Abbott.
No. 87 on War Dead List.
Son of Harry Edmunds Crute and Gertrude Mary Crute of Daison, Torquay.
Husband of Jean Crute, who was killed in the same incident.
(see Civilian List)

Peter Guy Francis 1041 20 yrs
Royal Marines   2nd Lieut.
Died at Royal Victoria Hospital, Boscombe (24th May).
Son of Dick and Doreen Francis of Hendon, Middlesex.
Buried North Cemetery, Plot A4/90, W.G.C. Headstone.

John St.Aubyn Jewell   Lt. R.N. (Retired) 68 yrs
Temp. Lieut. RNVR. H.M.S. President.
Died at The Central Hotel.
Of St. Aubyn, Mill Hill, London N.W.7
Son of Robert and Eliza Jewell, husband of Eliza Louise Jewell.
Cremated 1st June. Ashes scattered North Cemetery.

Staff Sgt. Reginald Wilfred Miles 7624966 23 yrs
108 Coy. R.E.M.E. Bovington. Height 6ft.
Died at
Son of Harold and Ada Louisa Miles, of Middle Bourne, Farnham Surrey.
Buried Farnham (Green Lane) Cemetery.
Grave Ref, Section B, Grave 981.

UNITED STATES OF AMERICA

ARMY PERSONNEL

Samuel C. Arone　　　Private First Class　　　33150489
175th Infantry Regiment, 29th Infantry Division.
Born 1918.
Buried Madingley Military Cemetery, Plot E, Row 3, Grave 51.

James C. Ashford　　　T/4
175th Infantry Regiment, 29th Infantry Division.

Raymond J. Berwind　　　T/5
175th Infantry Regiment, 29th Infantry Division.

Stanley L. Bodziony　　　Private First Class
175th Infantry Regiment, 29th Infantry Division.

Harry L. Parker　　　Private First Class　　　33001777
175th Infantry Regiment, 29th Infantry Division.
Born 1911.
Buried Madingley Military Cemetery, Plot D, Row 3, Grave 79.

Tony Rellick　　　Private First Class　　　33150525
175th Infantry Regiment, 29th Infantry Division.
Born 1919.
Buried Madingley Military Cemetery, Plot D, Row 1, Grave 69.

LUFTWAFFE

Name	Rank	Age

Karl Schmidt　　　　　Unteroffizier　　　　　21 yrs
Fl. Ausb. Rgt.Nr 809
Died when shot down, crashing into the St. Ives Hotel, Grove Rd.
First Buried in North Cemetery, Grave H82, as the Unknown
German Airman, 809 3 Flg Austlo Rgt 32 (buried 25th May).
Later identified as Uffz. Karl Schmidt, of 15/SKG/10.
Born 19.01.1922 in Herne/Westf.
In Feb. 1963 his body was exhumed by the WGC and reburied at
Cannock Chase German Military Cemetery.

Eugen Streich　　　　　Unteroffizier　　　　　23 yrs
Giebelstadt Nr. L 436
Died when his aircraft wing struck a tree, upon landing whilst
returning from the Raid on Bournemouth.
He died in the Luftwaffe Hospital at Caen.

The Lansdowne, 1950
showing the remains of The Metropole Hotel

Lansdowne Crescent, modern day

Royal London House (The Metropole Hotel site)

Debenhams, The Square Bournemouth
(formerly Bobby's)

Beales Store,
modern day

Bristol & West House,
modern day
(Central Hotel site)

GLOSSARY

SKG is the abbreviation for Schnellkampfgeschwader (fast bomber flyers).

The Luftwaffe Geschwader can be compared to the R.A.F. Group.

The Gruppe is the equivalent of a Wing, and the Staffel, a Squadron.

The Gruppe is identified by the Roman Numeral e.g. **IV**/SKG/10

The Staffel is identified by the Arabic Numeral e.g. **15**/SKG/10

Comparative Ranks:

Group Captain	Oberst
Wing Commander	Oberstleutnant
Squadron Leader	Major
Flight Lieutenant	Hauptmann
Flying Officer	Oberleutnant
Pilot Officer	Leutnant
Sergeant (NCO)	Unteroffiziere

Pilots leading staffels held the positions of

        Staffelführer (temporary position)
                      or
        Staffelkapitän (permanent position)

These were positions and not ranks.

                Katschmarek - Wingman

BIBLIOGRAPHY

Basil Collier: *Defence of the United Kingdom, Official History of the Second World War.*
Pub. Imperial War Museum (1994)

M.A. Edgington: *Bournemouth and The Second World War.*
Pub. Bournemouth Local Studies (1994)

Joseph H Ewing: *29 Let's Go!, A history of the 29th Division in World War II*
Pub. Battery Press (1948)

Johnathan Glancy: *Spitfire (The Illustrated Biography)*
Pub. Atlantic Books (2008)

Chris Goss with Peter Cornwell and Bernd Rauchbach: *Luftwaffe Fighter Bombers over Britain (The Tip and Run Campaign 1942-34)*
Pub. Crecy Publishing (2003) pages 243-255

Ted Hughes: *Bournemouth Firemen at War*
Pub. Dorset Publication co., (1991) pages 123-126

Winston G. Ramsay: *The Blitz, Then and Now. Vol. 3*
Pub. After the Battle (1990)

Nicholas Redman: *Marriott Bournemouth Highcliff Hotel*
(in-house publication)

Graham Smith: *Dorset Airfields in the Second World War*
Pub. Countryside Books (1999)

Vera Smith: *So much sadness, so much fun (R.A.F Ibsley 1942-1952)*
Pub. The R.A.F. Ibsley Historical Group (1997)

John Sweetman: *Bomber Crew (Taking on The Reich)*
Pub. Abacus (2005)

Jim Wilson: *Bournemouth's Carlton Hotel (A Century of Service)*
Pub. R.W. Associates (1999) Page 47

Newspapers

The Bournemouth Echo
24th and 25th May 1943, 12th April 2005.
The Times 1943
The Daily Telegraph 1943

REFERENCES

<u>Bournemouth Central Library</u>

List of Air Raids Warnings 1943 (ref. U769 224)

The Alphabetical List of War Dead

Bournemouth Corporation War Dead, Civilian and Military Register (Book 1) and Civilian Register (Book 2) (ref. U769 224)

The Scrapbook of wartime newspaper cuttings.

Letter from The Controllers Office, to The Mayor dated 18.11.1944.

Buildings and Other Areas Requisitioned in Bournemouth During World War Two - Compiled by the staff of Lansdowne Library.

Angela Beleznay: The R.A.F. Ledger of George Scott and Son (2008)

<u>Bournemouth Cemetery Office.</u>

The Register of Military Deaths 1914 to 1947 (also available above)

<u>The National Archive Kew</u>

RAF Ops. Book Ref: AIR/29/479

Air Raid Damage Report. HO 192/837

WEB SITES

Imperial War Museum
www.iwm.org.uk.

FW190 Orders of Battle
fw190.hobbyvista.com/oob.htm.

Famous World War II Planes,
http://www.geocities.com/CapeCanaveral/Lab/1688/GERMANS.

Kracker Luftwaffe Pilot Archive,
aircrewremembrancesociety.com/Kracker/KrackerArchive.

Iron Crosses of the Luftwaffe
www.aircrewremembrancesociety.com
www.raf.uk/bomber command

SOURCES

Combatants and Technical Specifications of Aircraft Page 74

Kracker Luftwaffe Pilot Archives.
Iron Crosses of The Luftwaffe.
Air Crew Remembrance Society.
Friends of New Forest Airfields.
Chris Goss "paper 29", Luftwaffe Fighter Bombers over Britain.
Famous World War II Planes.
Spitfire by Jonathan Glancey.

Civilian Dead Page 129

The Register of Civilian and Military War Dead.
The Alphabetical List of War Deaths.
The Hampshire List of Civilian War Dead - The War Graves Commission.
Sources not in the public domain.

Military Dead Page 146

The Register of Service Deaths – Bournemouth Cemetery Office.
The Register of Civilian and Military War Dead.
The Alphabetical List of War Deaths.
The list of Commonwealth War Dead.
The unpublished memoirs of Harry Mears.
AFAC, Ottawa.
The Aircrew Remembrance Society.
Sources not in the public domain.

PHOTOGRAPH ACCREDITATIONS

Every attempt has been made to secure the appropriate permissions for the illustrations reproduced on this book including where owners and copyright holders are different concerns. If there has been any oversight we will be happy to rectify the situation. Written submission should be made to the Publisher.

Many of these illustrations were originally published in the *Bournemouth Times* and both Bournemouth Reference Library and the Echo have had copies in their archives.

Page
- 6   © M. Shnider
- 11   (top & bottom) Natula Publications
- 12   (top) © Shamrock & Rambler
- 12   (bottom) © A. Beleznay
- 13   Natula Publications
- 14   (top) Echo, (bottom) Bournemouth Reference Library
- 21   (all) © W. Wenger
- 22   (all) © W. Wenger
- 24   (top) Bournemouth Reference Library/Echo
- 24   (bottom) © R. Coles via Aircrew Remembrance Society
- 30   Natula Publications
- 31   (top) Bournemouth Reference Library/Echo
- 31   (bottom) Bournemouth Reference Library
- 32   Echo
- 35   (top) Bournemouth Reference Library/Echo

35	(bottom) Bournemouth Reference Library/Echo
36	(top) Bournemouth Reference Library/Echo
36	(bottom) Bournemouth Reference Library/Echo
37	Home Office
38	(top) Bournemouth Reference Library/Echo
38	(bottom) Bournemouth Reference Library
43	Bournemouth Reference Library/Echo
48	(top) Home Office
48	(bottom) Home Office
49	(top) Bournemouth Reference Library
49	(bottom x 2) Home Office
50	Bournemouth Reference Library/Echo
51	(top) © J. Gear
51	(bottom) © T. Hughes
59	© Hopkins
76	© Mrs. Nippa
77	(top x 2) Aircrew Remembrance Society
77	(bottom) Aircrew Remembrance Society
89	(top) © W. Wenger
89	(bottom) © W. Wenger
90	(top) © W. Wenger
90	(bottom) © Mrs. Nippa
91	(top) © W. Wenger
91	(bottom) © W. Wenger
92	(top) © W. Wenger
92	(bottom) © W. Wenger
113	© R. Taylor
114	© R. Taylor
117	© R. Taylor
121	© R. Holloway

128   © A. Beleznay
152   (top) © C. Milner via Kinson Historical Society
152   (bottom) © C. Milner via Kinson Historical Society
153   (top) © Clarke via Chris Goss
153   (bottom) © Clarke via Chris Goss
154   (top) © Clarke via Chris Goss
154   (bottom) © C. Milner via Kinson Historical Society
155   (top) © Clarke via Chris Goss
155   (bottom) © C. Milner via Kinson Historical Society
156   (top) © A. Beleznay
156   (bottom) © A. Beleznay
164   (top) Bournemouth Reference Library
164   (bottom) Natula Publications
165   (top) Natula Publications
165   (bottom) Natula Publications
166   (top) Natula Publications
166   (bottom) Natula Publications